Unquestionably, Dr. "Dee" Since I met her several years ago, she has always exemplified to me an unwavering belief that the Word of God is not just a written word to be read, but that it is *truth* meant to be lived. I have observed her apply her faith in situations that would ordinarily seem impossible, but hers is no ordinary faith. "No Limits." Her example of true faith has been both an inspiration and an encouragement to me in my walk with the Lord, solidifying my belief that through an unyielding faith in God surely *all* things *are* possible.

After reading her personal experiences of faith and how God is truly a rewarder of those that diligently seek Him, I believe that your level of faith will go beyond anything that you ever dreamed possible. Thank you, Dr. Greathouse, for sharing this experience with us all.

—Lee Roger Jones
Bible Teacher
Living Word Bible Fellowship Outreach Center
S.D. James Evangelistic Association World Wide Inc.

What About ME?

What About
ME?

DELPHINE (DEE) GREATHOUSE ●

CREATION
HOUSE

WHAT ABOUT ME? by Delphine (Dee) Greathouse
Published by Creation House
A Charisma Media Company
600 Rinehart Road
Lake Mary, Florida 32746
www.charismamedia.com

Unless otherwise noted, all Scripture quotations are from the King James Version.

Design Director: Justin Evans
Cover design by Nathan Morgan

Visit the author's website: www.deegreathouseministries.com

Library of Congress Cataloging-in-Publication Data: 2014
International Standard Book Number: 978-1-62136-787-1
E-book International Standard Book Number:
978-1-62136-788-8

While the author has made every effort to provide accurate telephone numbers and Internet addresses at the time of publication, neither the publisher nor the author assumes any responsibility for errors or for changes that occur after publication.

First edition

14 15 16 17 18—987654321
Printed in Canada

~

*This book is dedicated to all those who had faith
and courage to trust God, especially in adverse
situations and circumstances. He is the best of us all!*

*To the family of the Donor who gave so much
so that I could live: may God always smile
upon you and grant you great peace.*

Thank you!

~

TABLE OF CONTENTS

PREFACE

F ROM THE BEGINNING, we were created in His image and likeness. Our very blood is His blood. Our hearts beat to the melodic symphony of His love pouring out into our lives in streams of goodness, beating in unison with the flow of God's own Spirit.

How do I know these things? Because interwoven in His love for me is His sustaining revelation given by the Spirit of God to those who execute the faith He has planted in their minds and hearts.

The birthing of life comes explicitly from the mind of God, and that mind is the cumulative power ignited by His Word. Before anything else, *God is,* and He is the sustaining power of all that exists both in the visible and invisible realms. In His variegated wisdom, He put Himself in all of us to ensure that we are never too far away from His loving hand.

When I see my future, I see God—not just the Father, but the Son and the Holy Spirit. I see them in my present as well as in my past. My daily strength, my hopes, dreams, and aspirations are inextricably linked to the life-sustaining force that governs all the ordinances of the universe.

Amazingly, in our minds we think we have all the time in the world, but the simple truth is we have what God has meted out to us. Time is relative to God's divine plan for this dispensation—and no one else's. Our opinions and plans will always substantially lack when juxtaposed to God's will.

I believe one of the truest shortfalls of humanity is that we forget our greatest self. Our intrinsic value in the Earth does not come from our material possessions or our successes in life; it comes from the riches and abundance of our divine qualities. Our spirit is the greatest asset that we possess, yet every day we let everything in our natural existence dictate who we are. Talk about a massive identity crisis: there are billions in the world today who are truly clueless. What do we do for security? We latch on to every identifiable influence we can—whether it be marrying the wrong person, pursuing the wrong career, having the wrong friends, or developing unnatural or unhealthy lifestyles, and the list goes on and on. All of this is a sacred cry for help. Yet the source of relief is buried in the nooks and crevices of our own hearts and minds.

Might I make a suggestion at this time? When you start searching for your true self, go back to the Word of God. Go back to the Creator. He created you by His Word; He sustains you by His Word; and all that you and I will ever be is intimately woven into His Word.

Long before the beginning of our lives was the Word. The Word was with God, and the Word was God! And we, my dear friends, are byproducts of that magnificent Word! Shall we begin?

ACKNOWLEDGEMENTS

WHERE DO I start when my heart is full of so much gratitude? I'm alive, and I'm alive in Jesus. Appropriately, I shall start with God the Father for giving me such an incredible life. There was so much I did not understand, yet You sent Jesus (God the Son) into the world not only to be the propitiation for my sins, but also to heal me from all sickness and disease.

I would be remiss if I did not celebrate God the Holy Spirit as well because, even when I was not listening, He was still talking to me! Thank You, awesome God; You have worked all things out for my good.

To my seed in the Earth, my daughter Teana; and my grandchildren Jessica, William (TJ), and Miles: the world is waiting to see how your greatness will impact the lives of God's people. Always remember that without God you can do *nothing,* and in and with Him, you are an unstoppable, creative force. I pray you keep that down in the soil of your heart so that you will be strong always and never let your human frailties get the best of you. I love you with the love of Christ Jesus, and I leave a legacy of lessons learned.

To my son-in-law William Sr: thank you for looking out for me, especially during my recovery...I really enjoyed our daily movie reviews!

To my brothers Leon, Arthur, and Vincent (Kip): we are all of the lessons Mom and Dad taught around the dinner table. Teach your children so that they may teach the world. I love you.

Thank you, Living Word Bible Fellowship (Roger and Janis Jones), for showing me that true friendship is built on the foundation of truth and that truth is the embodiment of God's Word.

To Karen Hill, for showing me that true friendship never stops loving, no matter how badly it's treated.

To my comrade Shelley Jesses, you were a lifeline sent by God Himself in the midst of my storm. Live long and prosper, my brother. Linda Jesses, thank you for looking out for me!

To the prayer warriors (Ambassador Cynthia Jackson, Mary "My Mary" Whitehead, Minister Eulinda Pickney, Minister Brenda Kelly, and Pastor Ray) who "stay on the wall" with me; God sees your labor of love for His people, and He will always take care of you!

To Pastor Bess, The New Commandment Church, Atlanta, GA: thank you, thank you, thank you for your encouragement at 2 and 3 a.m. when I would call or text during my midnight hour—you are my brother.

To Co-Pastor Anne McKoy, The Greater Faith Holiness Church, Durham, NC: thank you for telling me, "You know, maybe this is God's way of healing you." You are an amazing sister.

To Minister Yvonne Strachan, Ministries in Motion, Miami, FL: what can I say except you are a brilliant star, and I'm so glad God showed me your worth to His Kingdom and made you my sister by the heart. I love you.

Thanks to all the teachers, staff, and students at Pointe South Elementary School and Edmonds Elementary. You don't know how you kept me going all those years, especially keeping me focused on the students and all of your prayer requests. You made me a better vessel for God! (Hey Judy, you taught me something anyway!)

To Ms. Croy, Clayton County Public Schools: thank you for your support, especially during my recovery.

To Dr. Butler, Brenda, Sondra, and Jewell: you guys *rock!* Thank you for preparing me for the unexpected...Doc, four hours in your chair was too long; now I dislike Cream of Wheat!

To Dr. Jon Hundley, Dr. Johnson, and the entire Piedmont Transplant Institute: I salute you in the name of Christ Jesus for letting God use your lives and talents to bring healing to so many who are in desperate need. Your level of expertise and competence are exceptional. Thank you *so* much, Ms. Quinn, Caroline, and Tadzia.

Thank you, Piedmont Fayette Hospital Staff and Internal Medicine, Dr. Grybowski and Dr. Khandelwahl.

To Ms. Alfreda (Piedmont Fayette): you make my day every time I come in to have my blood drawn. Your hugs are priceless.

To Dr. Dollar and the World Changers Family of Believers: now I see the "changes" needed in this world, and I am confident with Christ's help, I can *change* something!

To Joy of the Lord Church, Inc, Hollywood, FL: you will always be my family.

To New Generation Missionary Baptist Church, Opa-locka, FL: you are by far one of my all-time favorite houses of God to minister in. You always let the Holy Spirit have His way. Keep being hungry for the Lord.

To Moon Man, the Moon Stars, and the Godby crew: the world should take note of you. You really inspire me to give my all. "Pain is weakness leaving the body" in more ways than one. Thank you, and I love you all.

Thank you, A2Z Imprints, for seeing what I see and making it happen.

To Tanisha Bess: you are an amazing graphic artist. I appreciate your worth.

To Vonnia Davis, let God use all of your gifts to bless His people—your eye in photography is extraordinary!

And how could I forget Jacksonville Theological Seminary for educating some of the brightest minds in ministerial history?

Thank you all who prayed for me and experienced this journey with me. My God has done *great* things.

INTRODUCTION

I N THE PAST, I would pray to God hoping that He would hear me, when I knew so many others were also calling His name. Often I was trying to figure out ways to manipulate Him to get what I wanted. I did not consider that He might just say no to my wants—and like a good Father, give me what I needed instead.

After many seasons of success, challenges, heartbreak, and failures, I finally grew up in God. I arrived at a place where second guessing and doubt were no longer commonplace. This book is about my journey and how I came to discover that it really isn't just about me; it is about God's incredible patience with the ones He truly loves, His children.

As an expression of that love, He sent Jesus into this Earth to show us that life is not an easy journey, but that it always fulfills the plan of the divine. I'm not saying it is God's will that we should suffer, but because sin exists, sickness exists—and wherever sickness exists, death is ever present.

Yet, we have hope, not just as mere humans, but as divine creatures operating as benefactors of God's grace. That grace through Christ Jesus is afforded to every believer in Him. That grace is part of the eternal structure of the triune God's existence. Yes, grace, like God, is eternal.

Christ came to Earth in the fullness of power and grace. All the fullness of the godhead, the totality of divinity, is represented in the body of Jesus, the Incarnate Word of

God. Within that fullness abides life, and the byproducts of the life force are health and healing. God's provision was made clear through Jesus' life and ministry in the Earth: wherever sin abounds, that much more does His magnificent grace abound—more grace than you or I could use up in a lifetime.

Do you realize that millions walk around every day broken, sad, and unaware of the benefits of being a child of the Most High God? We all have done things in this life that we are ashamed of. I truly believe that most of the pain we have caused to others or ourselves was because we had no idea of the true divinity inside us.

We have clung to our cultural roots; the things we learned in school and at home, from friends and even enemies, had lasting and influential relevance in our lives. We began early playing roles that never seemed to fit our persona properly, and we graciously followed what our hearts and minds picked up from what was determined to be societal norms.

Role-play is fun and exciting when everyone is doing it. What happens when one day you stumble because you see or hear something out of the norm, like Moses and the burning bush? Are you like most—never turning aside to see what it is? Or do the noises of the mundane drown out the subtle whisper? Maybe you are like me, wondering, *what was that?... that was odd...* And then you hear it again, a remarkable conversation which seems to be coming forth out of thin air.

Where is this warmth coming from that has overshadowed my entire being? Am I losing my mind? You ask yourself. The voice you hear replies, "No not yet, but if you continue down this path, you will lose much more than your mind." Just like that, you realize that you are not talking to yourself; it is Someone much greater.

At that moment, Jesus has brought grace and introduced it to your heart. The mind may not comprehend what is taking place, but grace always has a profound impact on our hearts, even the most wretched. For me, it took something *big* to transform my life from the darkness and trappings of this world and turn me into someone God can use for His glory.

Our lives are not ours alone; we are inextricably linked together by a common bond of love and creative authority. God alone reserves the right to give and to take life, and the ebb and flow of our lives are centered on our response to the things He allows within the process of His divine mind and will.

We are always challenged to choose life. These mortal bodies cannot live forever, but we are living souls, and our spirits do live forever. We choose whether to live by the ordinances of this world that will one day pass away or by the ordinances of the Kingdom of God that can never pass away. God says, choose *life*.

This means not only life in eternity but life in abundance here on Earth. Perhaps you regard abundance as material possessions, but to God, abundance is so much more. It begins with believing in Jesus Christ unto salvation, eternal life—and divine health and healing. We have become so acclimated to sickness and disease in our society that when someone is healed from a life-threatening illness, people are amazed.

Here is a question for you, why was Jesus never sick? Why is it never written that He became ill? You might say, "Because He was God." Yes—but He took on the physical attributes of flesh and blood, and flesh and blood gets sick because of sin. Jesus knew no sin, but He took upon Himself the attributes of sinful flesh. Yet, He did not allow His flesh to delve into sin.

At the appointed time, He took the sin of the entire world upon Himself on the Cross; the enormity of that sin crushed His flesh, and that flesh gave up His spirit. But you can't kill deity, and you can't destroy eternity. Jesus rose from the dead with all power over sickness, death, and the grave so that we as believers could do the same. Jesus is the fullness of the Godhead, the Father, Son, and Holy Spirit combined; therefore, before He took on the likeness of man, He already had power over sickness, death, and the grave. He came to give us that power.

Because Jesus gave us power over sickness, death, and the grave, we too can walk in divine health—not to see death, but to transition from Earth to life in eternity where there are no graves to hold us down.

I asked the Lord recently, "How can we walk and live in divine healing to the degree that there is no sickness or disease in these mortal bodies?" His first word to me was "Obedience." The second word was "Believe."

As a result of all my life experiences, I have learned to walk in the light of God's perpetual love for me. It is by far the most consistent and compelling thing in my life. God's consistency and faithfulness cause me to trust in His will, so I believe everything He tells me, and I desire never to disappoint Him. Every day I get up with a heart toward obedience, following His leading through the Holy Spirit.

There are days I fall short—because of my humanity, not because of the divinity of my spirit. I know God is inside me, leading me and cheering me on like my natural parents used to do when they were still alive. So I ask for forgiveness, and God reminds me that all of my sins and shortcomings—past, present, and future—have already been forgiven. There is no more condemnation for those who are in Christ; it was finished when it was nailed to the Cross.

I know I don't have to beat myself up about the wrongs that I have done because I am aware that grace is a magnanimous gift given to me by God, and with it I can live an abundant life free from sickness and pain. Society calls what happened to me a second chance, but I choose to call it grace in motion, propelled by God's eternal love for me!

Believe in God's eternal power; believe it can work for you. Let grace come in and usher you out of that sickness you are in. *Step out* from death's darkness into the liberating *light of life*. Jesus is the resurrection and the life. My friend, you too can *live and not die*.

Chapter 1

BORN IN PURPOSE

W HILE DRIVING HOME from a breakfast gathering today, I had an opportunity to reflect on the conversations that I was having with various attendees. I realized that as I began to tell portions of my healing testimony and the uniqueness of my relationship with God, they seemed more and more intrigued. One gentleman even replied to me, "You've got great faith," more than once.

As I played the conversations back in my mind, the Holy Spirit began to speak to me; He began to open up a new view of my purpose. Even though God had shown me things about my future, today's revelation seemed quite different. I meet people all the time; yet, lately there seems to be a gravitational pull that draws them and their attention toward me. "What is it?" I began to inquire of the Holy Spirit. He simply responded, "Your purpose."

He began to reveal to me that my life was designed to draw, teach, and encourage; to give from my gifts and talents; to serve, bring hope, and be a light in a world of darkness; to do what I was created to do; and to be a mouthpiece for God. He created me to stand before people as an epistle people can read, a testament to what God has done through and for my life. The Holy Spirit called it, "Born in purpose."

People often tell us to "live on purpose"; however, that's not it at all. Purpose is not to be put on, like some garment. Purpose is not acquired by any environmental influences in your life. Where you were born, who your parents are, where you attended school, your economic or social status—none of these define purpose. All of these things are external influences, but they were never created to be the driving force behind our purpose.

Purpose is the state of actually pursuing who you were created to be. Purpose is internal, the navigational pull and directives that come from the inside, not the outside. Purpose is the heart's energy source, and it is driven by the Great Revelator Himself, God Almighty. Purpose is a well-established position given only by God, even before you or I were placed in our mother's womb. You and I were purpose before we became anything else.

We all were a thought, a formulated creative design, with a specific function, existing in the mind of God. That thought from the mind power of God, formed into a spirit, possessed all of God's attributes. This creative being was designed with a purpose that only it could fulfill.

When the creative mind of God moves in power, it does not create outside of purpose. Everything created by God was purposed by God. It had purpose before the tangible creation ever manifested. The light had purpose as did the darkness, the sun as well as the moon, the tree as well as the grass. *Purpose* is the reason all things exist.

I was born in purpose. When God wrapped flesh around my spirit, He wrapped it around the embodiment of God's *purpose*. I am the tangible, visible form of God's thought. That means you and I have great value because God never makes any junk! Even more exciting, when we can't figure out what our purpose in life is, God always knows!

As the Holy Spirit began unveiling this for me, I began to understand why God told the Prophet Jeremiah, "Before I formed you in your mother's womb, I knew you" (see Jer. 1:5). Then God further explains to the prophet, "I know the thoughts that I think toward you, thoughts of peace and not of evil, to give you an expected end" (see Jer. 29:11). He is committed to bring you to and through all the things He created you for.

I believe there is a distinct difference between living on (your life being physically supported by purpose) and living in (your life being enclosed or surrounded by purpose). Purpose is inside of you; not all things in your life or your surrounding environment are supportive of your purpose. Some things are distractions, and they can send you on detours. Detours by their very nature are designed to take you away from your original route, with some degree of delay. Fortunately, for the believer, God will ultimately intervene and direct you back to purpose.

Now, in purpose, the indwelling Holy Spirit gives you the ability to see yourself in the future and to make choices that will enhance your path of destiny. In this way, you walk the path that God's own Spirit has laid out before you, asking for divine guidance all along the way. That, my friend, is purpose.

Do you realize that being born in purpose makes all your dreams and aspirations possible? Your spirit understands the leading of the Holy Spirit, and it yearns to do what it was designed to do. It always desires to advance toward what God created you to be. Why do think it makes you feel burdened and sad in your spirit when you acquiesce or are boxed into a role that you really don't want? Your own spirit desires to break out and be free.

You were not designed to role-play nor were you designed to veer into someone else's destiny. No one else was designed to veer into yours, either. I would agree that some destinies run parallel, but the beauty is in the melodic harmony of life's rhythm. It allows each individual creation to flow in harmony with all creation, even though they have their own distinct sound, much like the keys on the piano or the strings on a violin.

All of us, as we work within our designed purposes, are actually making a congruent sound which represents God's creative authority, working by design in a harmonious symphony. It works in a little space of eternity, which we call time, and that space has Alpha and Omega (the beginning and the end) in it. Let me ask you, how precious is *time* to a life well spent in *purpose?*

Now that you have some idea of what purpose is, may I have the privilege of taking you on a roller coaster ride with me through the last 17 years of my life? I would like you to see how God used everything in me to manifest to me why things happened the way they did, which brought me to a place of acknowledging who and what I am to God.

Let me put this disclaimer in from the outset. I, like you, have human emotions, yet sometime in my youth I quickly learned that my emotions cannot control what is really happening, or going to happen, to me. Instead, my perception of what is happening has an impact on how I walk away from or through what is happening.

I attribute it to how I was wired, how I was created. I really want you to understand this because the ensuing pages will give you a bird's-eye view of some of the things that I have been through, yet I never got mad with God, or asked Him, "Why me? What about my needs? What about me?" In my weakest hours and during the most difficult times, I could feel His presence and hear Him speaking to me by His Spirit.

I can only imagine all the complaining I might have done while He was using life events to draw me closer to

Him. The events were never designed to bring me harm, but to lead me to a place of maturity and trust in His purpose, will, and plan. I had to understand His divine purpose inside of me. I still exist today because He purposed for me to exist. For me, there is no *purpose* outside of God. When the doctors thought I would die, He told me to *live*. God told me, "Daughter, I think about you all the time. What do you think about Me? What about our relationship? *What about Me?*"

Chapter 2
GOD'S CREATIVE POWER

T HE FATHER DESIGNED each of us, not out of the dust of the earth as He did the first Adam, but as the consummated spirit beings that we are. He wrapped us as He did His own Son, in flesh. Moreover, I have discovered under the tutelage of the Holy Spirit that each spirit is uniquely designed in accordance with a specific purpose.

In other words, we are triune beings, designed and created by the God of all creation Himself; in the mind of God, there is always absolute certainty. There are no *oops!* or mishaps.

The problem we have is in understanding what God's creative mind and authority purposed when He created us. To be in the midst of God's creative authority is to be in the midst of His creative thinking and power. It is to understand His forethought and His manifold wisdom.

He created beings who never existed before out of the symmetry of His multifaceted thoughts with likeness to Himself and yet as intricately and uniquely designed as any snowflake. Divine and human, spirit and flesh, supernatural and natural: We were created with individual characteristics, propensities, thought patterns, emotional applications, 3.2 billion character traits, and divine revelation, wisdom, and power.

With His creative authority, the Father gave us life and eternal life, but He gave each of us His creative gifts as well. It goes far deeper than our abilities to comprehend, create, or develop; we can see beyond the natural realm into the supernatural realms, even to the point of making prophetic utterances of future events.

There are many more such gifts—like ministry, teaching, giving, ruling, and mercy. These creative gifts given to us directly from the Father bring a heightened level of existence in our world.

I am always amazed when I see people who have no real clue who they are or who God created them to be. I have spent many years on this journey of discovery, wondering who I am and what my purpose is. The knowledge of who I am is more profound than even I could have imagined. There is only One who can answer the question, "Why am I here?" That is God Himself, in the divine, congruent counsel of the Godhead, the Father, Son, and Holy Spirit.

All of our gifts, the natural and the supernatural, were designed by God to work in complete harmony with God's divine plan for humankind. Each individual, creative being was created by the will of God for a specific purpose. We must come to realize that His purpose will never change.

God is an immutable God; He changes not! From the beginning, in His own sovereign counsel, He decided that you and I would exist. From the sands on the seashore to the clouds in the sky and every created thing in between, in the creative authority of God, there has always been a divine purpose. God never creates for the sake of creating; there is always purpose behind His creations.

Even though God's thoughts and ways are higher than ours, we can rest assured that, whether we have come to the place of understanding God's will for our lives or not, it will *never* negate the truest fact: that God created us and placed us here in this earthly realm with *purpose* in us and *purpose* for us. Now I'm sure you are asking the big question: how do I find out what my purpose is? The answer to that question is quite simple, my friend: go back to the Creator.

Remember, before you were formed in your mother's womb, you were known in the mind of God and created as a spirit. God then took that spirit and, just as He did with the second Adam (Jesus Christ), He sent your spirit from heaven at the appointed time. He wrapped you in flesh, kept counsel with you in the womb, and then brought you forth as the apple of your parents' eye. You were an apple in your Heavenly Father's eye long before you were an apple in your earthly father's eye. Amen.

So everything we do, and how we do it, is already perceived by God. That is why Jesus continuously makes intercession for us. He prays for us, He makes request of the Father on our behalf, and then the person of the Holy Spirit coaches and counsels us to bring us to a place of maturity, in order that we may have an understanding of the things and the expectations of God. Who knows the mind of God better than His Son or His own Spirit? His Son is the expression of His love made manifest to us by His Spirit in us. "Who can escape the counsel of the Most High, when My own indwelling Spirit keeps you alive? Before I created the Earth for you to inhabit, you were alive inside of Me!" says the Lord.

Chapter 3

THE DIAGNOSIS

T WENTY YEARS OF military service is a very long time, especially when you relocate every two to three years. Yet I would not trade that experience for anything in the world. There are many things I have seen and enjoyed from the outset of my military career until my retirement in 1998. My experience in the military was life changing, and it had a profound impact on my life. In 1996 while in the military, something greater affected my life—and that greater thing will go with me to the end of my earthly experience.

Being a divorced, single mom had its share of challenges; however, I enjoyed being a mom and a soldier. We were stationed at Fort Rucker, Alabama; I was an instructor and writer at the US Army Warrant Officer Career Center. Life was good. I was rapidly approaching my twenty-year mark and looking forward to a great future. I was still contemplating whether or not I would remain in the service for another five to ten years. My daughter was a sixth grader at this point, and I had to make decisions concerning both of our futures.

I had gone in for my annual well woman's check, and I told my doctor about a pain I felt from time to time on my right side as well as the flow of my monthly cycle. My doctor scheduled me for an ultrasound, and I traveled to the nearest Air Force base and had it done.

A few weeks went by, and my doctor called me in for a consultation. As I sat across from her, she informed me that the ultrasound revealed I had a small cyst on my right

ovary. She informed me that was of little concern: however, the ultrasound had revealed something else that *was*
a concern.

The ultrasound revealed several cysts in my liver and on
both of my kidneys. Being optimistic, I asked her if she
could give me a pill for it. Unfortunately, she said there
was no known cure for polycystic kidney and liver disease.
She went on to tell me what the prognosis was: I would
have complete renal failure by age 78.

I thought that was good news, considering I was only
35 at the time…who cares about 78, right? She told me
to do some research, and in the days ahead, we would
monitor closely my blood pressure because that was key
to prolonging my kidney functions. My doctor asked me
if I desired to see a psychiatrist since I had received some
devastating news. I told her no; I was fine, and everything
would be okay.

During the remainder of my tour at Fort Rucker, a
number of unfortunate events began to occur. I began to
get such severe headaches that one night I was rushed to
the emergency room; there I discovered that my blood
pressure was sky high.

What I did not understand at the time was that the cysts
on my kidneys contained urine, and the excess weight of
the cysts caused my kidneys to work harder. Because they
had to work harder, my blood pressure spiked, thereby
causing me to have to take medication to keep my blood
pressure at a safe level (even though that level had now far
surpassed my old blood pressure).

Even when it was time for me to be reassigned to
Atlanta in the fall, the doctors still had not found the right
combination of medicines to stabilize my blood pressure.
Additionally, I noticed my abdomen was getting a little

pudgy. At this point, I continued to do my daily sit-ups until they became impossible to do.

The Army transferred me to Atlanta in November of 1996. I bought a home and began to work in my new position as law office manager for the Judge Advocate General at Fort McPherson. After months of being at Fort McPherson, it seemed as though the doctors had finally found the right combination of medicines to control my blood pressure, and the dietician had me on a strict low protein diet in an effort to control and preserve my kidney functions. They even sent me out to a civilian gastroenter-ologist (liver doctor) and a nephrologist (kidney doctor). I had no idea this would be the beginning of a long and impactful relationship.

Have you ever been in a place in your life where you never expected to be? You know, just playing out the hand that life has dealt to you, be it good or bad. Not certain at all where the windings roads are going to take you, but you do know right in that moment it's the clearest path that you see. That, my friend, would be me in the ensuing months and years, trying to grapple and understand. What was this place God had put me in? Why, when I looked around, was no one else in that place, but me?

I quickly learned to adapt to my surroundings. My abdomen was slowly expanding, and my uniforms were not fitting properly, nor could I do some of the athletic things I had done in the previous nineteen years. My world was changing rapidly, sometimes faster than I was adjusting. I was on a daily regimen of medications, limita-tions in my diet, and now limitations in what I could do physically. It seemed the momentum was shifting, and it was not in my favor.

It was time to look at my life, at the value and the

contributions I was able to make in my current situation, and decide whether I should remain in the military. I loved my job, and I loved being a soldier. I had worked my way up in rank from a private to staff sergeant; then I changed ranks and became a warrant officer. Yet the truth of the matter was, I was evolving into someone else, and I began to feel that someone else had too many restrictions and limitations to be the stellar soldier that the Army deserved.

You see I had spent my entire adult life in an institution that was far superior (with the exception of God) to anything I had experienced in 36 years of living on this Earth. The Army had been good to me and my family, and every day I gave the best of me because I believed that life was worth fighting and dying for. That competence was not a fad, but a way of life, and courage was not the absence of fear, but something greater that was calling me to action. My resolve was simple: if I could no longer be all that I could be in the institution that taught me so much about inner strength and sacrifice; if my physiological capacities were diminished to the point that 100 percent was no longer possible, then I with a heavy heart would have to retire and say goodbye.

I had enlisted in the Reserves at age 16 and joined the regular Army before my eighteenth birthday. After crying, reflecting, and being honest with myself, my comrades, and my country, I retired after 20 years and one month to pursue a career in corporate America as a project manager.

In May of 1998, I retired from the United States Army and spent the next 17 years working as a project manager, hospitality manager, and subsequently an educator. During these seventeen years, my abdomen continued to grow. My gastroenterologist at the time was convinced that eventually it would stop growing. So I continued to buy big blouses and kept my nose to the grindstone.

Several years went by, and in February of 2005, my mother was diagnosed with lung cancer. She lived in Hollywood, Florida, and in March she underwent surgery to remove two lobes from her right lung.

I was flying back and forth from Atlanta, taking her every 21 days to chemotherapy. She completed her last treatment in July. In August, I had come home from work, and God told me to move to Florida to be with my mom. I did not question Him because I really wanted to be there to take care of her, even though the cancer at this point had been totally eradicated. I obeyed, found a job in West Palm Beach, and moved from Atlanta to Hollywood to be with my mom.

My first day at work was September 15, 2005. Much to my surprise, by November 2005, my mother was dead. Words cannot begin to express my emotional turmoil at the unexpected loss of my mother. I was devastated. Before I go into my account of that season of my life, it would be appropriate for you to understand what really happened to my mother.

I would like to explain to you how God deals with me when I write. On most occasions when I sit down, the Holy Spirit begins to speak to me and I write. I have in my possession notebooks of things He has said. Months before I began this book, the Holy Spirit had me sit down, and He began to tell me the details of my mother's death. When I began to type, I began to hear my mother's voice so clearly. When you read the ensuing chapter, it will be my mother speaking and not me. I was not there at the time of my mother's death; I was working, and I probably could not tell it like she could. I only have the memory of that tragic day. I will return in Chapter 5. *(Please note: Some of the material in the following chapter is very graphic.)*

Copy of the local newspaper, November 5, 2005—
the morning after my mother's death

Chapter 4
MURDER ON 24th STREET

I T IS THE first week in November. Today is Thursday, and I have several errands to complete. I need to go to the bank, pick up a few things from the grocery store, and I feel inspired to visit some old friends today. It has been storming here for weeks in South Florida. Well, what do I expect? It is hurricane season.

Katrina blew through New Orleans and tore that city apart; I guess we are fortunate that Wilma wasn't so devastating. Our lights are still off on my end of the street, and I am getting tired of taking cold showers and eating by candlelight every night. Maybe by tomorrow the lights will be back on. If not, I'll go back up to the hotel where my daughter is working and spend the weekend with her.

It's now seven o'clock, and my daughter calls me like she does every morning at seven. As we talk, I mention to her the dream I had last night. It kind of disturbed me because in it my stepfather, Pop, dies right there in his front yard. My daughter suggests that the dream might be a warning to me that Pop was going to die soon.

This is what really disturbed me, though: I tell her I could smell death in my room when I awoke. My daughter asks me, "Are you sure?" I tell her, "Yes"; it was a smell like I had never smelled before. I go on to elaborate that in the dream, when Pop fell in the front yard, he lost all of his bodily functions. When I awoke I could smell that same smell in my bedroom. My daughter then tells me not to fret myself, that God will reveal it all to me in time. We then end our conversation, and I focus on the errands I have to run.

I better make sure Pop has enough food at his house to carry him through the weekend, I think. *I'm sure the neighbors will check on him from time to time for me. Reminder to myself: when the grass dries, I must have Daniel the next door neighbor come over and cut my grass; it's getting pretty tall.*

When I arrive at the bank, the line for the ATM is pretty long, but the line for the inside tellers is worse. I see Maxine while I'm waiting in line, and she can tell by the look on my face that I am getting pretty impatient with the slow pokes in line. Maxine and I greet each other, talk for a few minutes, and I finally get my turn at the ATM. After saying my goodbyes to Maxine, I head off to complete my errands.

After spending most of the afternoon visiting with friends, I stop by one of my best friend's house to have fish with him and his family. They have been staying with their father because their lights were off due to the hurricane as well. As the evening gets late, they insist that I stay over until the morning, since my lights are also out. However, I decide against it; it would be best to return home to see about my stepfather who lives a house away from me.

I can't explain it; I just feel a sense of urgency to get back home. So I depart and head back to my home in Hollywood. When I arrive home, I check on Pop and then go home to take another cold shower.

It is about 8 p.m. when my daughter calls me, and we talk and laugh for about 45 minutes. I tell her the lights are still off, and I will come back to spend the weekend at the hotel in West Palm after my nail appointment in the morning.

While my daughter is on the phone with me, her cousin calls her from Houston. When she tells him she is on the phone with me, telling me I shouldn't be in the house with the lights off like that, he tells her to tell me, "That's right, Auntie, because it isn't safe." I just laugh it off.

I had grown up in this particular neighborhood all my life—and not until I got married did I move to Fort Lauderdale. I lived in Fort Lauderdale for over 30 years with my husband, raising our four children. However, I had moved back to Hollywood within the past three years to tend to my aging parents. So I assured the two of them I was more than safe in my neighborhood—besides, everyone knows everyone here. It's one of those neighborhoods where there is a church on every corner, and the local mom and pop store has been there for generations. You know, quiet, peaceful, where folks still come home and sit on their porches.

Yes, there were many days since my daughter had moved back home, that we sat on the porch sipping lemonade, and reminiscing about when she was a child and her summers spent on this same porch with her grandmother, who went to be with the Lord a year ago. Yes, the air is still clean, the grass still green, the neighbors sit and chit chat with you, and the birds sit on the power lines singing sweet melodies. Now what could possibly happen in a neighborhood like this?

After my phone call with my daughter concludes, I receive a call from my dear friend Mackie. He is checking to make sure I arrived home safe and that I am tucked in for the night. He too voices his concern that I should have stayed with him and his family until morning; nonetheless, I am home, and I feel safe because I have my God and me.

I turn my cell phone off to preserve the battery because my house phones are all cordless, and they need to be plugged in to work. I read a little bit of my Bible before I blow out the candle and drift off to sleep.

After being asleep for a few hours, I am awakened by a startling noise coming from the area of the living room. I live in a quaint, two-bedroom bungalow; the living room isn't far from my bedroom at all. I am not quite sure what the sound is because I was asleep when I heard it, but because I am a light sleeper, it doesn't take much to arouse me.

I immediately jump up and proceed to my bedroom door; it is difficult navigating because the house is pitch-black. I can't see a thing. As I make my way from the side of my bed to the door, a man comes in the door; he immediately grabs me and begins to punch me in my face. I can tell from grabbing him that he is a small framed man, a little taller than me, but not by much. As I fight him with my hands, I can feel something wet on his arms; I can only assume it is blood. I cannot see very well; my eyes are still adjusting to the darkness.

The man begins to punch me in my stomach, and he knocks the wind out of me. I stumble back against the dresser at the foot of my bed. He keeps hitting me over and over again. I am getting tired of throwing punches back at him and scratching him. Months before I had surgery to remove two lobes from my right lung due to lung cancer. I have spent weeks in rehab and chemotherapy. I am cancer free, but I am not as strong physically as I used to be. I realize I am fighting for my life, so I give him all that I physically have to give.

After a few moments of fighting in the doorway, he hits me suddenly in the head with a huge glass pitcher which was sitting on a stand with a basin by the door. When it breaks, I immediately go down to the floor. Surprisingly, during this time something amazing happens to me; my spirit actually leaves my body. Yes, in an instant, I am no longer on the floor as a three-part being. Because God has

has separated my spirit from my body, I can feel no pain at all. My spirit is elevated now above the events that are transpiring on the bedroom floor, and I can see the man clearly now. It is my next-door neighbor, Daniel—the one who had done odd jobs for me around the house to make some extra money from time to time.

But what is happening to me? Why is Daniel there beating on me, and why am I now up toward the ceiling, looking down at Daniel while he continues to punch me in the head? He is like a mad man, crazed, incredibly strong, and out of control. Blood is pouring from his arms, where he cut himself when he climbed through the front window. I am bleeding also from my head, mouth, nose, and hands. I am trying my best to get up from my knees, but he is relentless. I feel myself weakening; he is beating me with all of his strength.

Daniel somehow gets his feet tangled in the extension cord by my bed. As he reaches to untangle his feet from the cord, he snatches the cord from the wall and wraps it around my neck. I am screaming, "Don't! Don't!" Then he punches me again. As my spirit continues to look on, I see the cord cutting through my skin as my brain is slowly deprived of oxygen. I begin to black out. As he squeezes the cord tightly around my neck, there is no more fight left in me. I fall face down on the floor at the foot of my bed.

Realizing that death is imminent, I begin to plead with the Lord—not for me because my spirit has already been separated from my body. I know it is time for me to go meet my King. I am pleading for my daughter, who loves me dearly. She might be the very one who finds me. Lying in a pool of blood, with my final breath, I ask the Lord, "What will happen to my daughter? Will my daughter be okay? Please, Lord, take care of my daughter..."

I died that day. In my bedroom, my favorite place, at the foot of my bed, in the company of the angelic host about 4 a.m. in the early morning hours of Friday, November 4th. My spirit takes flight, and my mortal body closes it eyes. Indeed, the spirit of death has waited all day Thursday and until the wee hours of Friday morning in my bedroom to claim its next victim.

Daniel never looks back nor does he hesitate as he goes back and forth walking across my now lifeless body, while he transports my purse, CD player, DVD player, and flat screen TV out the back kitchen door, next door to his house, just before daybreak in two black garbage bags dripping with my blood and his.

Some of you reading this book might say I died a horrible death, because when innocent blood is shed, our society calls it murder. Ironically, isn't that the same thing that happened to Jesus? Jesus' blood gave me a new life in eternity because of the blood He shed for humanity. Even though a lot of my blood was shed in my bedroom, and I departed this life, I'm alright. I have no pains and no worries. The world may forget my name, but because I'm a believer, let's just say my name is now written in the Lamb's Book of Life!

To my children, grandchildren, and great-grandchildren, remember: each of you have a piece of me resident inside of you. "And ye now therefore have sorrow: but I will see you again, and your heart shall rejoice, and your joy no man taketh from you" (John 16:22).

My mother, Christeen Jones-Davis (November 26, 1939–November 4, 2005)

After this I beheld, and, lo, a great multitude, which no man could number, of all nations, and kindreds, and people, and tongues, stood before the throne, and before the Lamb, clothed with white robes, and palms in their hands; and cried with a loud voice, saying, Salvation to our God which sitteth upon the throne, and unto the Lamb. And all the angels stood round about the throne, and about the elders and the four beasts, and fell before the throne on their faces, and worshipped God, saying, Amen: Blessing, and glory, and wisdom, and thanksgiving, and honour, and power, and might, be unto our God for ever and ever. Amen. And one of the elders answered, saying unto me, What are these which are arrayed in white robes? and whence came they? And I said unto him, Sir, thou knowest. And he said to me, These are they which came out of great tribulation, and have washed their robes, and made them white in the blood of the Lamb.

—REVELATION 7: 9–14

Chapter 5

PRELUDE TO BROKEN

Bom Bom Bom Bom... *Where is that god-awful sound coming from? Oh, the alarm is going off.* As I sit up, confused thoughts bombard me. *Where am I?...Boy, I was having a nightmare. I dreamed...Where is this sick feeling in my stomach coming from?* I feel sad and confused. *What is this on my chest? Oh, it's a picture of Mom, godmother, and Auntie Martha. Wait a minute, that was no dream; my mom is dead. I feel like vomiting. Oh my God, I can't stop the tears; let me get to the bathroom and wash my face. Too late.* "Oh mommy, mommy, mommy, why did someone do this to you? How could anyone kill someone as good as you?" Sobbing uncontrollably. Breathing erratically. I've got to get myself together before I wake up the entire house.

I want to see my mom. I took the coward's way out; I couldn't bear to see them bring her out of the house in a body bag. What am I going to do now? I've never had to live without my mother; she's been with me all of my life, and now, somebody killed her like a coward in the night—but why? The police asked me if someone had a motive for killing my mother. Who would do such a god-awful thing? I feel sick; I race to the bathroom, vomiting profusely—my head hanging in the commode. I don't know whether to cry or just keep vomiting. Lord, please help me. My soul longs to just hear my mother's voice; I can't hear anything except my own heart crying out in anguish and despair. Did she suffer? What happened to her? How long did she lay there before she died? Was she in pain? Did she think about me or my brothers? The vomiting continues.

I should have been in the house with her. I could have helped her fight. I should not have left her alone; she was my heart, and now she is dead. Momma, I'm so sorry I was not there with you. What happened to you? God, how could you let such a horrific thing happen to my mom? Tell me...how did she die? What happened to her? Sobbing.

I hear a bedroom door opening. *Get yourself together; get your head out of the toilet and wash your face. You must go to the airport soon to pick up Karen; she's flying in from Atlanta this morning, remember.* As I look in the bathroom mirror, I realize I look just like I feel, sick inside. I wash my face again and proceed out of the bathroom into the den of my godparents' home. My godmother is up, but she looks like she has been crying all night. "How could this happen to Chris?" she asks. I don't comment; I just look at a picture I found of my mom and godmother when they were much younger.

My godmother looks at me with tears in her eyes and says so plainly, "I can't help you with this one, Dee; I need somebody to help me." As much as those words hurt me, somehow I know exactly how she feels. I have no expectations of her at all because, at this point, I have no expectations of myself.

Life in its own precarious way has just dealt me the blow of a lifetime. I am not sure, at this point, if I will ever recover; all I want to do right now is to die too. My mother and I had such a special relationship because I was the only girl, and I have three brothers. She was mom, big sister, and confidant all rolled up in one. Less than 48 hours ago I was talking with my mom, and now her lifeless body is on the examiner's table at the coroner's office as the investigation continues surrounding her untimely death. An active murder investigation seems so surreal to me. This could have easily been a page that was taken from the script of CSI. The only difference is that it is not drama. This is real life; it's a story about victims, my mother, my family, and myself have become the victims of a brutal crime, and no one seems to have any answers for me right now.

As I sit in the den, I begin to have flashbacks of yesterday, the worst day of my human experience…It was 7 a.m., and I called my mom like I usually do when I am not at the house with her. I had been staying at the hotel in West Palm Beach where I worked as the Director of Housekeeping. The hotel had sustained damage from Hurricane Wilma, and I was required to get my staff up and running early each day because we still had guests coming in and out of the hotel. So I stayed in a room there in order to avoid having to commute in the early morning traffic.

When I called my mom, she did not answer; I assumed she had not turned her cell phone back on yet. I waited an hour or so for her to call me, but when she didn't, I called her again. It immediately went to voicemail. I really didn't think anything was strange at the time because I was busy giving my staff their assignments. At about 9:30 a.m., I called my mom again; still I got no answer. About 9:45, I received a phone call from my cousin, who lived across the street from my mom. She asked me if my mom was in West Palm with me; I told her no. She then began to scream uncontrollably, "You need to get here right now! The police are all over the place. Your mom's car is in the yard, and there is a body inside the house!" Then she began to yell continuously, "Cousin Christeen, Cousin Christeen!"

I immediately hung up the phone, called one of my

younger brothers, and told him to get to momma's house. "Something has happened," I told him, "And whatever you do, don't let them move her until I get there." I then called my godmother and told her to get to my mom's house: "Tell them you are her sister, and don't let them move her." After that, I called my oldest brother who was en route to Chicago to visit his in-laws. I proceeded to my room to get my car keys. When I retrieved my keys, I stopped for a moment and began to talk to God. I said to Him, "God, whatever this is, please give me the strength to handle it."

For a moment I stood there, reflecting on the moment when my mother awakened in ICU after she had surgery to remove the lobes from her lungs. There she was with a tube in her chest extracting blood and water. I remember vividly sitting there watching as the tubes separated the water and the blood from her lungs. When she opened her eyes, I was there smiling, telling her she was going to be fine. They got all of the cancer, and I was going to be right there. She nodded her head and went back to sleep.

In the ensuing months, I traveled back and forth from Atlanta to Florida to take care of my mom, while she recovered after getting out of rehab. I was there for her first chemo session, and I was there for her last chemo session. I even slept in her bedroom in the same bed with her at night, when she finally was able to come home. She didn't know it, but there were many nights I was up just watching her breathe, making sure her chest was rising and falling properly. I prayed over her and watched her sometimes until I fell asleep myself. I fixed her meals, made her soy shakes, watched television with her, and sat on the porch with her drinking lemonade.

When I moved back to South Florida, everything seemed to have fallen right in place. I landed the perfect job and increased my salary by $20,000 dollars a year. Even though for a period I was commuting back and forth from West Palm to Hollywood, I had found a house I wanted to buy in Boca Raton, which cut about 20 minutes off of my commute time. Things were looking pretty bright, and I had decided to enter into the contract for the house, which was being built and would be ready by late January. But right now, I needed to get downstairs and inform the HR Director that there was a problem at my mom's house.

Chapter 6

BROKEN

Brokenness is not a permanent state of being. It is a place of transition—a portal designed to move us from one place in destiny to a more perfect state in the mind of God!

A FTER MY MOTHER'S untimely death, I was shattered like a precious vase broken into a thousand pieces. Two weeks after her death, I tried to return to work and proceed with a normal life, but there was a problem: my life was anything but normal. Not only was I continuously dealing with my physical problems and the effects of polycystic liver and kidney disease, but now death had left its aura over my life.

One of the hardest things to do in this immortal / mortal life is to push through the darkness of mortality and make it to the light of immortality. The grief of my mother's murder left me weak with no physical strength. My mind was telling me to press on, yet I found myself gasping for every breath I was trying to take.

I had a staff of 40 employees to manage, and the one thing I knew I was good at seemed to be a fleeting memory. Something life-changing had happened to me, and I kept reaching for my old self, my familiar traits and attributes, the ones that had paved the way for a successful military and now civilian career, but I was grasping at memories.

I felt so displaced. I could not live at the house my mother and I had shared for the past two months; the job I had transferred to was unfamiliar to me now, and the tragic stench of death was sucking the life out of me, both day and night.

I could not eat; I could not sleep; I could not laugh; and my tears cut a new wound in my heart and mind every day. I ached when I walked, and I ached when I talked. I could not see the future because the Valley of Death was much too consuming.

I had prayed the morning I received the call about my mother; I was at work because I had spent the night there the night before. When my cousin called me, I ran to my room, got my keys, and paused for just a moment. I asked the Lord, "Whatever this is, please give me the strength to handle it."

Yet here I was two weeks later, struggling more than I had after the initial shock that someone had murdered my mom. The pain was so great I asked the Lord, "Why didn't you let me die too? Why wasn't I there fighting with her?" In the midst of my inquiry, I acknowledged that only death would soothe my pain. Everyone I knew to talk to was hurting too. Who could I go to that would help take the weightiness of the pain away? Who had answers for me? My long- time confidant was dead. My prayer partner was dead. My mentors were all dead. Why was I still alive?

To me the shortcut to peace from all the pain and suffering was death. My boss called me in with the HR Director and told me he needed the old Dee back to manage the staff and to keep things in order. I will never forget that day in the conference room as I sat across from him at the conference table. I looked him in his eyes and told him, "The old Dee died on November 4th, and she is never coming back.

He looked at me in utter disbelief while the HR Director just nodded and lowered his head. The HR Director had driven me the morning of my mother's death from West

Palm Beach to Hollywood, because he felt that if something had happened to my mother I was in no shape to drive.

He saw everything I saw that day. Three houses roped off with crime tape, the CSI team in their white suits, police cars around the perimeter, and hundreds of people, family, friends, neighbors, and onlookers. It was like something taken from the pages of a story line straight out of Hollywood, only there were no actors present that day, just victims.

After about 30 minutes in the midst of all that chaos, the HR Director asked me how I could be so calm, knowing that the body lying inside my mother's house might very well be hers. I looked at him and simply said, "If that is my mother in that house, and I believe that it is, she prepared me all of my life for this day."

My mom was my rock here on Earth because God allowed her to give me all of my moral training. She taught me about truth and pure love. She would often tell me and my brothers, "Don't tell me you love me; show me." She didn't do a lot of hugging and kissing because she wasn't raised that way, but we knew she loved us because she always made sure she and my dad provided the best for us.

When I was nine, my dad's sister died of kidney failure at 27 years old. A month later, her husband died in a tragic automobile accident. They had two small boys, a five year old and a three year old. My mom then vowed that her children would not grow up helpless, unable to take care of themselves, so we all learned how to wash, cook, iron, clean, and do the dishes.

There were many lessons taught to us about pride, strength, character, and self-discipline. She taught us to never let our weaknesses be exposed. She believed the world would use our weakness, whether it was momentary or not, against us, and we had so many hurdles to cross before this life was over.

Christeen was her name. Before I was five years old, I had to know how to spell it and my own name as well. She taught me how to tell time at age four using an old alarm clock. She had taken the face off so she could move the hands. Funny how those things stay with you forever. I can tell time on any type of time piece whether they have numbers, tick marks, or just the hour and minute hands, just like reading and spelling; I've been doing that since I was four. I entered first grade at five, wearing my Cinderella Timex watch because Christeen invested a lot of *time* in me!

You want to know what happened with my boss? He asked me what I wanted to do. I told him I wanted to fill up my car and drive northbound on I-95 as far as it would take me. Three days later I put in my notice to leave. During those three days, I decided to get some sort of direction for my life. Since God wasn't going to let me die just yet, and I'm much too big of a coward to kill myself, I needed a plan.

Now some of you might ask, with your upbringing in the church and your knowledge of God, why didn't you just ask Him for the plan two weeks before? Let me try to explain. This was not the first time in my life I had dealt with death. My father had died seventeen years previously, and my grandmother who was my prayer partner had died the year before my mother. Losing a loved one is hard in itself. Losing a loved one to sickness or natural causes leaves you in a totally different frame of mind than when the loved one is taken from you by a thief in the night. The first face outside of heaven that represented love to me had been brutally beaten and strangled to death; that takes loss to a whole different level.

The natural being grieves because of its emotional state of being. While in this state, it wrestles with the spirit man which always moves toward and in the things of God, and it has a different agenda. At this point in my life, I knew the Lord, but I did not have a viable relationship with Him. That makes all the difference in the world.

Sometimes tragic things happen in life; yet, in every tragedy some good, some hope, some joy, and a whole lot of growth comes. I have often said, though my mother's death was tragic, it was also by far one of the best things that has ever happened to me. The gravity and despair of the pain that I was suffering as a result of her loss made me turn aside from every material thing, every prideful thought, every selfish desire of my flesh, everything on this earth that mattered to me, including my own life. Yes, I turned, took all of my attention and all of my affections and crawled back from that place of darkness to the one true light: God the Father, God the Son, and God the Holy Spirit.

I crawled in my prayers and wept in my brokenness until I found myself resting at Jesus' feet. As my hands touched His feet, I reached up, touched the throne, grabbed His garment, and held on with all of my might. He reached down, lifted my head, and said to me, "I am the Lord thy God, that healeth thee. Make a decision and walk sure-footedly, knowing that I am with you wherever you go." In that moment, in that space of eternity, I became aware that I had to be in Christ Jesus in order for the broken pieces of my life to start coming together again.

I never knew that at His feet was love beyond compare. At His feet it was alright to be broken and wipe away all the war paint of life's challenges. At His feet were consolation and the answers to all the questions my heart yearned to know. At His feet I could no longer feel the aching of my heart because His presence takes away all pain and replaces it instantaneously with everlasting joy. There is no suffering, no sickness, and no pain at His feet. I understand now why His mercies are new every morning because for every single day of challenges that we face, God provides His unmatched grace, and that grace issues out the necessary mercies for the varied situations that come our way. Without grace, the free unmerited favor of God working on our behalf every day, we would never be victorious over our past failures, disappointments, or tragedies.

His grace is even far more reaching than that because it allows for healing and restoration of the soul. It gives us a new perspective if we would just let go of the hurt and pain, grab hold of His hand, and not let go. It's really our own choice. Do we let the past hold us captive until it chokes the very life out of us? Or do we reach with all the strength we can muster toward the light of our future, the promise of life?

Yes, I did it too. All I had left of my mother was the pain, and I wore it like a badge of honor because I felt if I didn't cleave to it, I was betraying her somehow. I was a good daughter, and I loved my mother deeply, but my love could not save her, and that was a hard thing to live with. Yet, after being in Jesus' presence, I realized that was not a burden I was ever supposed to bear. My friend, you can never have an encounter with Jesus and come back from that encounter the same.

Time is also important to the healing process. Yet, we must be willing to go the distance in time. No matter how overwhelming life may be, from the first day of impact until the days that follow, the sting of the pain diminishes with the dawning of each new day. No, I'm not saying you will forget it; what I am saying is that, for me, no matter how hard I try to recapture the raw emotions that I felt the morning of November 4, 2005, I can never recapture that surreal feeling, nor the intensity of the pain. Time in the Lord has taken the sting away.

Now I understand why Paul wrote in First Corinthians, "O death, where is thy sting? O grave, where is thy victory?" (1 Cor. 15:55). My mommy believed in Jesus Christ, and she has the victory. How do I know? Because Jesus Himself said, "I am the resurrection, and the life, he that believeth in me, though he were dead, yet shall he live. And whosoever liveth and believeth in me shall never die. Believest thou this?" (John 11:25–26).

Chapter 7

FORGIVENESS

In order to truly experience the mercies associated with forgiveness in our own lives, we ourselves must be willing to forgive.

T HERE ARE MANY times in life when things happen that are so horrific, so devastating, that we think we will never recover. There is one thing I know for certain: no matter how severe our circumstances are, we do have the strength to overcome. That, my friend, is not a quixotically conjured-up thought, but a truth, because in everything that will ever come our way, good or bad, God has granted to each of us the necessary grace to overcome it.

The real problem occurs primarily because most people are unaware of this amazing provision of grace. In the previous chapters, I recounted the events that occurred when my mother was murdered. All of you are wondering I'm sure what happened to her assailant Daniel. Well, Daniel died, seven months after my mother, while sitting in jail awaiting trial. Daniel died from complications of AIDS. Yes, Daniel had AIDS in the early morning hours of November 4, 2005, and yes, he was bleeding from the cuts he sustained when he entered the window he had broken. I remember the bloody trail that led to my mother's bedroom—blood on the sofa, on the carpet, in the hallway, the stain from the bloody puddle at the foot of her bed where she died, the blood spattered on her dresser, and the trail of blood that was on the kitchen floor that led to the back door—but I remember the day I forgave Daniel just as vividly.

January of 2006 is when I really began my journey toward healing from the devastating circumstances of my mother's untimely death. I had returned to Atlanta because the memories and pain were too great for me to overcome while trying to pick up the pieces of my life and continue on. Every day I was in Florida was a struggle.

When I returned to work a week after my mother's funeral, I could barely walk. Every breath was labored; what I didn't understand at the time was that this was the burden, the weightiness of the grief I was feeling. My heart was broken; my life was fragmented, torn in itty bitty pieces. I told myself to keep moving. My mind was pushing me, yet physically I was carrying the grief in the core of my very existence, and my flesh was feeling it all.

I lasted in South Florida until the end of December 2005, and on January 1, 2006, I drove a U-haul truck with a remnant of my shattered life in tow back to Atlanta. I initially moved in with my Aunt Connie, and a few days later she had a delightful house guest arrive. Her name was Mama Katie, and she spent exactly one week with us. On the very first day, she and I sat on Auntie's front porch, and it didn't take me long to realize God had orchestrated this divine meeting.

She was 90 years old at the time, vibrant, witty, charming, and when you looked in her eyes there was this twinkle, a whimsical illumination not common in men. Mama Katie was the vessel God used to teach me a profound yet practical way to forgive. I still use it today, no matter how slight or egregious the offense may be.

As Mama Katie and I sat on Auntie's porch for the first time, she began the conversation by telling me she knew about my mother's murder and how sorry she was for me and my family. The next thing that came out of her mouth was so unexpected it instantly offended me. She told me in spite of all of my pain I had to forgive my mom's murderer or I would never heal.

To me at that time, it was the most deplorable thing I could have heard. She didn't even know me, my mother, or my background. How could she tell me in the midst of my darkest hour to forgive that creature who had no regard for human life? I got angry.

As I looked at her, I glimpsed that twinkle again. I tried desperately to wrestle with my emotions. How could I in good conscience lash out at a ninety year old, when my parents had always taught me to respect my elders, even when I thought they were wrong?

She continued to tell me that true forgiveness is not easy, but the capability is in all of us. Then Mama Katie gave me a simple exercise to do. She said when I could do this exercise without unforgiveness and hatred in my heart, then my healing from the pain that held me captive would begin.

This is what she told me to do. She asked me if knew what my mom's murderer looked like. I told her, yes; I had seen pictures of him in the paper. She told me to bring the view of his face to my mind's eye, and when I could see him clearly, tell him, I forgive you. And when I could forgive him, then ask the Lord to forgive him too.

With everything in me, I wanted to say, "Are you crazy?" Instead I looked at her and said, "I can't do that right now." She told me she understood and reminded me again that my own healing would not occur until I found space in my heart to forgive Daniel.

It had only been a month and a few weeks since my mother's murder, and I was wrestling with a lot of thoughts about what had transpired with my mom. The truth of what occurred haunted me. My deep, abiding love for her was etched in my thoughts, and now she adds forgiveness.

I didn't want to forgive Daniel; it was my badge of allegiance to my mom. How could I betray her, forgive him, see his faults, see his brokenness, see his need, and love him, like Jesus had done for me so many times before? *Nooooooo,* my head screamed...yet my heart was flesh and not stone. God had sprinkled an agent of change called love over and into my heart, and that love, like a woven thread, was now stitching the fragmented pieces of my heart back together again.

Mama Katie went back to California after those seven days. I never saw her again, yet she, like my mother, left me with her indelible impression. In the ensuing days and weeks, I began to bring Daniel in my mind's eye, not without much struggle and a great deal of pain. At first I would just bring his face to mind...I could not muster a word of forgiveness. After a few weeks, I began to pray for him and myself.

I believe it was about a month after Mama Katie had returned to California, when I was doing my morning prayer, and Daniel popped in my mind. I saw him for the first time in his brokenness; I saw him worse off than me, and I heard my own spirit say, "I forgive you, Daniel." I could see his need for forgiveness was greater than my need for revenge.

My hope then was that God would forgive him. I said out loud, "Daniel, I forgive you for murdering my mother." I began to weep, and in my weeping I asked the Lord to forgive me for walking in unforgiveness. I asked that God would forgive Daniel, for he did not know what he was doing when he killed my mother; he was just an instrument used by the devil to steal, kill, and destroy.

Since my mother's death, I have grown not only in my walk of faith but also in my walk of forgiveness. Because of our sinful nature, we are prone to error, but God's unfeigned love toward us compels Him to see us as Christ saw us, worth forgiving and dying for.

How can we always walk under the blood-bought mantle of forgiveness and never understand that the counterpart of forgiveness is love? Just as the counterpart of unforgiveness is hatred. To appreciate true, undefiled love we cannot have an ounce of any of the byproducts of hate. A little leaven leavens the whole loaf. In other words, a little bit of unforgiveness (a byproduct of hate) in your heart makes the entire heart sick and unable to give or receive the truest form of love.

Over the years I have learned how to forgive a lot of people. I have come to realize that unforgiveness keeps me from truly loving, and that keeps me bound—yet forgiveness allows me to love, and love always liberates.

Chapter 8

THE WILDERNESS

D O YOU REMEMBER that after Jesus was baptized, He was led to the wilderness for forty days and forty nights? This was symbolic of the forty years the children of Israel spent in the wilderness. Interestingly, no matter how long the wilderness experience is, there are certain truths that this trying time always brings forth.

Depending on what God's plan is for your life, the time spent in the wilderness is in direct proportion to the birthing of the things of God which now must begin to manifest in your life. Most of us go into the wilderness kicking, screaming, and, if we are like Moses, running for our lives. However, once we get to the other side, we realize it was a necessary process.

My wilderness experience began when my mother was murdered. Up until that time I had a very good life, the usual bumps here and there, but nothing like the wilderness brought to me. The wilderness was a dry and barren place—not a place you wanted to travel through alone. Some company along the way might help; then again, company could be a distraction.

The wilderness is not a place to take up residence; it was designed as a passing through point just as brokenness is. The difference, however, is this: brokenness is a place of forgiveness, healing, and redemption. The wilderness, on the other hand, is a place of reflection, as well as identification with and submission to, the Deity. Again, neither place was ever designed as a place for us to stay, crippled and wallowing in despair.

There are a number of ways to be led into the wilderness, including following someone else there. Most times, however, the leading, even when you follow someone else is designed by God. God is there, and the devil is allowed access to you there as well. It is in the wilderness that Satan questions your faith and tempts you to question it as well. He questions who you think you are, to see just how much you know about God's plans for you. He even goes as far as making you doubt what the Word of God says.

Many have fallen and failed in the wilderness because the testing was so great and they were unaware of what the Word of God says about them. Many don't know the promises, and some who do still get caught in Satan's web of deception when they get to the wilderness.

This dark, barren wasteland is the place where all the junk in our lives is identified and then discarded. This is where we learn quickly what in us can be utilized by God. No excuses are allowed in the wilderness; all falsities, misconceptions, and misdirection are destroyed.

Indeed, it is the place where Satan loves to tempt God's people. Satan tempted Jesus in His humanity while in the wilderness because He knew He could not tempt Christ, the divine. Let's look at what Satan dared to say to Jesus, "If you be the Son of God…" How did Satan dare to say that to the One he knew was God's Son? Satan himself once resided in heaven with Christ; however, his true motives were to get Jesus in His humanity to doubt His identity, purpose, and very existence.

Yes, the flesh is weak, but the One who is greater is inside of us. God's Spirit is much greater than our mortal beings. Remember, the Spirit of God leads us into the wilderness, and the Spirit alone will bring us out. There is much to learn about ourselves in the wilderness, and after we have defeated fear, unbelief, and Satan there, God can then minister to us. We don't come out of the wilderness until we come out strong, having the ability to hear God, and the strength to do His will. No two wilderness experiences are the same; they are custom designed based on who you were created to be within God's creative authority. My wilderness experience took eight years to come through. After eight years in the wilderness, I would venture to say, my future looks pretty bright.

Here I am in November, the eight-year anniversary of my mother's murder and the eight-month anniversary since my surgery—*healed.* If you had asked me during the eight-year wilderness experience, "How are things going for you?" I would be the first to admit that, initially, because my grief was so great, I wanted to die. Today, in retrospect, it was the best thing that could have ever happened to me!

It made me seek after something greater than myself and greater than this world could give me. It made me find my Creator God; Christ, the great love of my life; and my best friend, the Holy Spirit. It was all worth it, and if I had to do it all over again, I would because it brought me to a place of great awareness. The sum total of who I am, experiences and all, are in His capable hands. *All of my faith rests in Him.*

As humans, we never want to go through anything uncomfortable, anything that takes us out of the familiar. Have you ever considered that the familiar could be a trap set to keep you in bondage to your own way of thinking? We never volunteer for the wilderness, yet if we keep living, we will eventually find ourselves in that most uncommon/common place.

Endure hardships as a good soldier because the breaking and the wilderness are definitely for our greater good…*Amen!*

Chapter 9

SICKNESS AND THE BLOOD

IF YOU DON'T remember anything else after you read this chapter, please take away one thing: there is always life in the blood. There are so many people and nationalities in the world, yet we are all part of one body, one family in God. We all have the same blood running through our veins; it might be a different blood type due to our DNA, but one thing is for certain: the same blood that flowed through our forefather's veins flowed through Christ's—and today it flows through ours. Without the blood, life would be impossible.

When I was hospitalized in August of 2012, it was because my blood had become contaminated. One of the cysts on my right kidney had ruptured and sent urine racing through my bloodstream. I thought I had contracted the flu, and for a week I endured chills, sweats, and fever. It was not until my breathing was affected and pain crippled me that I was taken to the hospital from the classroom of the elementary school where I was working.

I was rushed to the ER, and they began to draw blood and run tests on me. I was in excruciating pain and struggling to breathe; they began to give me oxygen and told me I had to stay calm. I was calm; even when I was gasping for air, my heart and mind were calm.

After an hour in the ER, the doctor came in to tell me I was a very sick woman; I had some sort of infection in my blood. What I did not know at the time was that the infection was killing me. I was transported upstairs to the Critical Care Unit where I would remain for the next two weeks.

Infectious disease, internal medicine, and nephrology were working frantically to figure out what was causing the infection. In the meantime, every six hours the nurses would come in with either morphine or Percocet for pain as well as a series of antibiotics in hopes of arresting the infection. The infectious disease doctors kept telling my daughter they had a positive and a negative, and they needed to get a match, which was two positives, to treat the infection. In other words, they continued to test my blood for a match, so they could treat the infection appropriately. On day two, thrash was forming in the back of my throat and mouth from the extreme doses of antibiotics, which caused me to have to rinse my mouth three times a day with horrible-tasting stuff called Nystatin. Who would have imagined this would become my new best friend for the weeks ahead?

The doctors finally discovered the cause of my blood infection and began an aggressive regimen of antibiotics; now I was in need of a blood transfusion. At this time, I had been hospitalized for about three to four days. My kidneys were failing. The internal medicine doctor asked me on several occasions, "Why is your liver so big?" Believe it or not, I wasn't concerned about my liver; I had lived with it protruding for over 16 years at this juncture. All I wanted them to do was figure out what was wrong with me, treat me, and send me home. I told the internal medicine doctor, "God will take care of my liver. Can you just fix what is making me sick?"

Nonetheless, one of my physicians ordered this amazing treatment to be done with my blood. They came in with a huge vial and filled it up with my blood. A courier came and, under lock and key, transported my blood to another lab at another hospital. I was told that when my blood came back from the lab, it would no longer be red. The lab would extract all of the white blood cells from my blood and send it back in a smaller tube. When the blood returned via courier, it would be milky white, and they would at that time put my white blood cells back into my body.

Even though I was under morphine, I realized there was something significant about the blood. Janis, a dear friend and fellow laborer in Christ, had called the hospital the day before and given me a word from the Lord. She had been praying for me without knowing the details of my situation—only that I had been hospitalized. God begin to speak to her concerning me. After Janis received the word, she called the hospital and gave me the word over the phone. I had one of the ministers who was visiting with me write the scripture down. This is what it said, "And when I passed by thee, and saw thee polluted in thine own blood, I said unto thee when thou wast in thy blood, Live; yea, I said unto thee when thou wast in thy blood; Live" (Ezek. 16:6). Again, Janis had no idea that my blood was infected; she just knew that I was in the hospital, very sick.

Because of my lethargic state due to the morphine, the true revelation of what was prophesied to me did not register until months later. Even now as I write these pages I feel the Spirit of the Living God as He speaks concerning the ministry and the power of the blood.

What is it about the blood? The atoning power as it relates to sin, the healing virtues that lie within: Oh, this blood gives us strength from day to day and never loses its power.

We are familiar with the blood of sacrificial animals used in the Old Testament as an offering for man's sins. We know about the blood smeared on the doorposts by the Children of Israel while in captivity in Egypt—and yes, we know about the atoning, redemptive power of Jesus' blood, which ushered in healing and deliverance from the penalties of sin and death. Yet, the indwelling Spirit of God wants to give us a closer look at *the blood*.

Why is blood red? Human blood is red because it contains a large number of red blood cells, which contain hemoglobin. Hemoglobin is a red-colored, iron-containing protein that functions in oxygen transport by reversibly binding to oxygen. Oxygenated hemoglobin and blood are bright red; deoxygenated hemoglobin and blood are dark red.

White blood cells (or immune cells) are cells which form a component of the blood. They help defend the body against infectious disease and foreign materials as part of the immune system. As well as in the blood, white cells are found in a large numbers in the lymphatic system, the spleen, and other body tissues. (The lymphatic system is part of the circulatory system, comprising a network of conduits called lymphatic vessels that carry a clear fluid called lymph toward the heart.)

The circulatory system processes an average of 20 liters of blood per day through capillary filtration which removes plasma while leaving the blood cells. *Plasma* is the

> ...pale yellow liquid component of blood that normally holds blood cells in whole blood in suspension. It makes up about 55 percent of the body's total blood volume...Plasma also serves as the protein reserve of the human body. It plays a vital role in intravascular osmotic effect that keeps electrolytes in balanced form and protects the body from infection and other blood disorders.[1]

---

1 http://en.wikipedia.org/wiki/Blood_plasma

As you can see from these brief definitions, God created blood with healing properties. I am amazed at all of the internal systems that were put in place when God created us. How could we ever consider that we evolved from apes with the superior intellect of God? Just think for a moment about how the mind power of God works: even with the 7.5 billion plus people inhabiting the Earth at this present moment, He knows each person by name, their eye color, shape, and skin color. He knows how many hairs are on each head. He knows when their birthday is, when their death appointment will be, and how they will enter into that death appointment. Greater still, He even knows all of the previous generations. He knows everyone who ever entered into the earthly realm, and yet, we have the audacity to question the Architect of the entire universe and insult His wisdom with the theory of evolution.

I can only imagine Adam as he stood lifeless before his Creator God, just a shell of dirt now formed as clay. Then a most intimate moment occurred when the Creator breathed into his nostrils the breath of life. In Him was life (see John 1:4), and He gave humankind that precious life that only God can give. In this moment, we can see God's creative authority at work.

During the process of Adam's creation, every detail of his existence mentally, physically, and spiritually was carefully crafted by God. All of the body's systems were formed meticulously. He created every detail of the circulatory system—from the arteries to each cell, including the route necessary for the bloodstream. Can you imagine? God even considered the dilation of the pupils to adjust to light and darkness, the moisture necessary to keep the cornea from getting scratched, and the formation of our tear ducts because He already knew how often we would cry.

The forethought of God is astounding to say the least. In His creative wonder, He gave us a heart, with valves and ventricles that direct not only the flow of blood, but life functions within the body. And He didn't stop with the heart. Not only does it support our physical life, it also feels pain and joy. The mind has the capability of delineating between what is a physical attribute of the heart and an emotional stimulant. The melody of the heartbeat was given to Adam when the same breath that breathed life into Adam, whispered simultaneously "I love you." Inside of each of us is the heart and the pure love of God. Why can't we see it and understand it? God's love was given in the First Adam and sealed for all eternity in the Second Adam, who was Jesus Christ, God's son.

> For God so loved the world, that he gave his only begotten Son, that whosoever believeth in him should not perish, but have everlasting life. For God sent not his Son into the world to condemn the world, but that the world through him might be saved.
> —JOHN 3:16–17

At the beginning of my second week in the hospital, physical therapy and occupational therapy arrived. I was really unaware that I needed their services; however, it was made apparent to me quickly. The nurses had been bathing me. I had a catheter, and I had been using the bed pan; my feet had not touched the ground since my arrival August 14, so I was unaware of what my limitations might be. Physical therapy gave me exercises to strengthen my body and helped me get to the point where I could at least wash myself up. However, occupational therapy was a different story. They sent a nice lady to me named Michele (I did not know it at this time, but she revealed to me days later that she was a liver transplant recipient); she came in the late afternoon to get me out of bed. She had a belt-like harness to assist in lifting me up. Of course I inquired as to why the belt was necessary, and she informed me that I would not be able to get up. She was right. When she pulled me up with the harness, as I stood for the first time in two weeks, my legs completely buckled. I could not believe I had no strength in my legs. The therapist had a walker next to my bed, and she assisted me in balancing myself with the walker. When she asked me how I felt, I responded with the short tune from the movie *Space Jams:* "I Believe I Can Fly." My daughter and those in my room gave me a big grin of encouragement. At the time, I had no idea this would be the beginning of a long journey, and God was up front leading the way.

After two weeks, I left the hospital again by ambulance, headed to rehabilitation. It was a gloomy day for me because I never imagined that I would end up in rehab, learning how to walk again. The rehabilitation center was filled with senior citizens; I was the youngest resident there at the time. They all stared at me when they saw me in the halls, wondering, "What is this pregnant lady doing here?" I felt so out of place, and I longed to get my life back.

It was very difficult for me to understand what God was doing, so I took it one day at a time. My new therapist came and took me down to the therapy room to assess me. He picked me up in a wheel chair, and I asked him if I could have a walker. I told him I had started to walk a little at the hospital under supervision, and I was confident I could do it at rehab as well. The therapist told me at that time he could not make me any promises; however, if I could complete every task he gave me that day, he would give me a walker and send me on my way.

You would be surprised at what can motivate you when you have the will and the courage to just try. All of the exercises that he challenged me with that day became the hallmark of my workout for the next ten days. Even though I was in pain, taking oxycontin and oxycodone, I was determined to get out of rehabilitation as soon as possible. I worked through the pain; I worked through the feeling of abandonment and uncertainty. This all was a Band-Aid; there were still some underlying issues with my health that had to be dealt with.

By the way, on my first day with the therapist, I finished all his challenges and left the physical therapy treatment room, taking slow, deliberate steps toward my room with my walker. (The next time I used a wheel chair was when my daughter came to pick me up; she rolled me to her SUV to take me to her home.)

During my stay at rehab, I had a daily routine I needed to adjust to. I started taking wash-ups in the bathroom sink because we could only go to the showers every other day. It was hard to stand up at that sink and wash from head to toe. I was extremely weak. They woke us up every day by 7 a.m., taking our vitals, giving us our medication. Then breakfast was served, after which we washed up or headed down to the showers. Thank God for sit down showers; I know I never could have showered on my own if I had to stand. When I emerged from the shower, the aides would lotion me down and help me get dressed. I used my walker and walked back to my room and rested for about an hour; then it was off to therapy.

I spent ten days in rehabilitation, and during this time, I had many unanswered questions. My thoughts were uncertain and unstable as I waved good-bye to my nurses; I was glad to be leaving. I felt the warmth of the sunshine on my face as my daughter was driving, and I took in the scenery that I had not seen upon arrival because I came by ambulance.

But I also wondered what the future had in-store for me. In this time of transition, what was God doing with me? I had waited for the past sixteen and a half years for God to heal me, holding on for dear life to His promises that He was the Lord God who heals. Yes, by Jesus' stripes, I was healed. I just didn't know how or when He was going to do it. It never crossed my mind—not this day anyway—that He could be healing me or even opening doors that no man could shut, just for me. For this moment, I was just glad to be leaving rehabilitation. I was too weary today to think too far ahead. I would leave that until tomorrow after I got some much needed rest with my family surrounding me.

Chapter 10

WAITING

What do you do while waiting between the promise and the blessing? Pray and be faithful and grateful.

ONE OF THE most difficult things for a Christian to do is to be content while waiting on the Lord. Learning to trust in His sovereign will to push us through the wait. Patience is key, but that patience comes with knowing that God's divine plan is operating in our lives.

That patience, however, is difficult at times because we can only see what is in front of us; it's hard to look beyond the pain and the suffering. And yes, the uncertainty and the unknown is difficult. Your mind is always questioning what is next…What is required of me to succeed? What is the plan? Is the plan close, or is it in my distant future?

So I entered a time when my understanding and my faith would be tested. When I arrived at my daughter's house from rehabilitation, my grandkids were glad to see me. They had not seen me in weeks; they knew I was sick, and they were accustomed to seeing me at least once a week, but they had only seen me once in the last month when I was in rehab.

I had my walker in tow and my pain medication. My thought process at this point was pretty simple: I won't be here very long because as soon as I get my strength back I can go back to my own place. So I settled into my granddaughter's room for what I thought would be a couple of weeks.

In the interim, I was going back and forth to see my internal medicine doctor; he was preparing my paperwork and recommendation to be reviewed by the transplant folks at Piedmont Transplant Institute. It didn't take long at all: I arrived at my daughter's the second week in September, and on November 2, 2012 I had my first appointment at the Transplant Institute.

I met my pre-transplant liver doctor, and he thought, after seeing my CAT Scan, that my insides were fascinating. He told me; however, that my condition was not good; I was suffering from malnutrition because my enlarged liver had displaced many of my internal organs, and transplant would be necessary in order to save my life.

At that moment, tears began to roll down my eyes for the first time during this entire ordeal. I knew I was sick, and I knew changes must occur in my condition, yet I never expected to hear I was dying from malnutrition. As I prepared for what was next, I knew God was with me and only He could deliver me.

This is a photo of me in rehab, September 2012, seven days after leaving the hospital.

As you can see from the photograph, after 17 years my liver had expanded to an enormous size. My doctor said it looked like I was carrying five full-term babies. It was an enlarged liver with hundreds of multiple-sized cysts. Additionally, I had two oversized polycystic (multiple cyst) kidneys as well.

What many of you may not realize is there is much preparation to be done in order to prepare a patient for transplant surgery. From the outset, it must be determined by a committee whether or not a person is a good candidate for transplant. When a patient like myself is sick and there are no other options to save their lives, transplant is available for a second chance at life. I want to share the process that I went through because there are many who desperately need transplant surgery, and they are afraid or don't have the necessary resources. Ultimately, they decline this life-saving option, or the lack of resources won't allow it. I can tell you this, the process takes courage and the will to live. I know by faith an individual can garner both of them.

EVALUATION PROCESS

An evaluation for a liver transplant involves having many tests, procedures, and visits with physicians. It also includes meeting with many members of the transplant team. All these consultations, tests, and procedures will help the doctors know if a liver transplant is right for you, and if any other treatment options are available. These tests also help them evaluate if a patient is well enough to have liver transplant surgery.

There are several components that must be in place to prepare for a successful transplant experience from start to finish. These are the team members that make it happen.

TRANSPLANT TEAM

The pre-transplant coordinator provides education regarding the transplant evaluation process, listing for transplant, and patient responsibilities before and after transplant. When you meet with the Pre-Transplant Coordinator, you and your family member or primary care provider have an opportunity to ask questions, get information, and address any issues regarding the evaluation and / or transplant.

A hepatologist is a physician who specializes in liver disease. The hepatologist assists in the medical management of your liver disease and works with the transplant team to determine if you are medically suitable for transplant.

A nephrologist is a physician who specializes in kidney disease. The nephrologist operates in the same capacity as the hepatologist, the difference being they care for the kidneys.

A transplant surgeon (you will meet him momentarily) discusses the appropriateness of the transplant based on the information obtained during the evaluation. The surgeon also discusses the risks of the surgery and the possible complications after the transplant.

A social worker will perform a psychosocial evaluation. During this evaluation, the social worker will help to identify psychosocial issues that could hinder a successful transplant. These issues include a lack of social support, financial support, or insurance, and a history of substance abuse.

A financial coordinator will work with you to help you understand your insurance coverage. It is important to understand the costs that may not be covered by your insurance or medical coverage.

A registered dietitian will perform a nutritional assessment and provide nutrition education to patients.

Some patients may need to be referred to another service for consultation; for example, many patients need to be seen by a pulmonologist (lung doctor), or a cardiologist (heart doctor) to assess other medical conditions.

THE TRANSPLANT OPERATION

During the transplant surgery, I was put under general anesthesia, which put me to sleep, blocked pain, and paralyzed parts of my body. I was also placed on a machine to help me breathe. The transplant surgeon made an incision across my abdomen. Through this incision my right kidney, liver, and gallbladder were removed, and a donated liver (without a gallbladder) and a donated kidney were placed into my abdomen. My surgery lasted eight hours.

There is a post-transplant team as well, which consists of the same type of team members to ensure you receive the best possible care and best possible chance to survive.

As part of the preparation phase for my transplant, I had to attend educational classes and support group sessions which included both pre-transplant and post-transplant patients. During these meetings I met a lot of sick people like myself; some were worse than others. Some had been waiting for years to receive an organ. By this time, I was so sick I could barely sit erect in a chair without hurting. I was taking pain medication every six hours, and at times it seemed not to be enough. All I could do was focus and keep my mind on the fact that God was in control, and somehow I knew I would not wait for years to pass by before I received a transplant.

The sessions were so beneficial because they gave specific guidance on all of the procedures, including what I should expect before and after transplant. I even got to see live footage of a liver transplant operation.

During this time, I had another problem I was dealing with as a result of end-stage liver disease. It was called *ascites,* a build-up of fluid in the abdomen caused by cirrhosis.

When most of us hear *cirrhosis* we automatically associate it with chronic drinking problems, but for me that was not the case. I was not, nor have I ever been, a drinker.

Cirrhosis is scarring in the liver after long-term inflammation or injury. It is caused by many diseases that affect the liver and is usually present in end-stage liver disease (ESLD).

I had to go periodically to the hospital to have the ascites fluid drained. The first time it was drained, they removed five liters of fluid. The second time, they removed four-and-a-quarter liters (see photo). Even with the drainage, I still had enormous extension in my abdomen.

Here is a photo of what the fluid looked like
that was drained from my abdomen.

Most of the nutrients derived from my foods, instead of being processed through the liver, were just floating around in my abdomen—which is why I had a life-threatening case of malnutrition.

As the weeks passed, I had to spend two days in the hospital getting a complete physical examination—lungs, heart, bone scan, blood work. You name it; I received it, including all my dental work. All my systems were a go, with the exception of my liver and kidneys. I could see even then God's hand on my life; although my kidneys and liver were extremely sick, my heart and lungs were as strong as ever.

It was now January 2013, and I was ready to be placed on the transplant waiting list for a liver and a kidney. Organs are allocated according to the policy of the United Network for Organ Sharing (UNOS), the national organization that maintains the organ waiting list. The livers are primarily allocated according to how sick a patient is. Being put on the waiting list for a liver or kidney transplant does not guarantee the availability of an organ or the certainty of receiving a transplant.

The MELD (Model for End Stage Liver Disease) is a score ranging from 6 to 40 that provides a marker for how sick your liver is. It also defines your place on the organ list.

MELD = Model End-Stage Liver Disease
GOOD 6 = 97% One Year Survival Without
    Transplant

15 = 85%

25 = 15% 5 out of 6 dead at one year without
    transplant

40 = < 1%

MELD diagram

Because I live in the Southeast, where they perform 100 transplants a year, a MELD score of 24 is typically the highest score. On January 17, 2013, I entered the list with a MELD Score of 22, which put me in the 85 to 99 percentile. My wait was coming to a close because God was doing something extraordinary in my life!

Just knowing He had taken care of every little detail made my mind automatically line up with His plan for me. God's mind is so intricate and fascinating! When you think you have considered all the variables, He reveals so much more that never crossed your mind.

That is why it is imperative that we trust in God. He sees so far ahead of our plans and thoughts for our lives. Sometimes the very thing that you never considered is the very thing He uses to bring you to that blessed place in Him. He always knows the plans He has for us, and every little detail, especially when He says, "You shall live and not die." As a consummate Creator, He knows what it will take to bring you and me to a state of total restoration.

So I ask you, how could I think about dying, when God was constantly bringing life every day before me to see? I spent a year at my daughter's house with her and her family. Most of my days were spent with my then two-year-old grandson Miles, and I found out quickly that two year olds have a lot to express.

In my wait, I realized how precious life really is. Just lean on death's door; you can feel the chill of emptiness and abandonment, when those around you who are busy living have no inclination what that chill feels like. Sometimes I would hug Miles just to feel what real living felt like. Living in the shadow of death makes you look at your mortality every day, and you quickly become aware that something has to quicken you to bring you back to remembering your faith in the one who is greater than anything you might face. The moment you identify with Him, your immortality kicks in and strengthens your mortal weakness, and then you can rest in the stillness of God's comfort until tomorrow comes and your faith is challenged yet another day.

I believe God strategically placed me in my daughter's house where the newness of life and innocence was present before me every single day. Yes, God has a plan long before you get to the place where you need a plan that will work out for your good. I know now that my life insurance, or should I correctly say, *assurance,* has truly been paid in full by Jesus Christ, the Anointed One and His Anointing. This inner knowledge allows you to rest in the wait even when sickness and death are all around you.

Chapter 11

MIDNIGHT HOUR

Why does the weakness of our humanity
always show up in the darkest of times?

W AITING ON A transplant is not an easy task. For many, it may take several years, depending on the MELD score and where the individual falls on the transplant list. I was blessed to land in the mid- to top range; however, depending on when organs came in and the compatibility margins, my wait could still be months down the road.

During the wait, I spent each day at my daughter's trying to take care of my two-year-old grandson while she and her husband worked and the older grandkids were at school. Most days it was a struggle because I was in constant pain, taking oxycodone every six hours. I learned quickly that once my grandson was up, I needed to feed him and keep him busy downstairs until we ate lunch. Then he knew, like I knew, that it was naptime.

For me, the trips to the transplant clinic and encouraging myself during the wait were the most difficult. My comrade Shelley (I refer to him as comrade because we are both retired armed services members) was always in good spirits when he would pick me up and take me to the doctors. He would always point me and my thinking toward the days ahead, when I would have my transplant and a brand-new start. Some mornings he would pick me up at 5:30 a.m. During the winter months it was very cold, and it took all of my strength to get dressed, go down those 15 stairs, and wait for him to come.

It's funny—I never believed I would be in this cycle of misery for a long time. I can't explain that except to say God's own Spirit inside of me knew the cycle had an impending point of conclusion. There were many days I would laugh through my pain, thinking of happier times that had gone by. I would look in the mirror everyday and see a shadow of who I used to be...it seemed as though I was fading with my own shadow.

I knew what the doctors had said: if I did not get the transplant, I would die of malnutrition because my liver had taken over the space of my internal organs, and they were not able to do their jobs well. My two-year-old grandson could eat more than I could. My daughter would fix my meals and place them in a saucer because that is all I could consume.

It appeared that the shadow of death had consumed all the brightness my life had transmitted over the years. Even though everything around me said, "You are dying," I was not ready to let go of the promises of Jesus and His healing power. I was not ready to succumb to the darkness; I was not ready to die.

God had revealed so much to me about my life at this point. I knew that He was a God who could not lie—so where were the manifestations of the things He had shown me? Where were the promises that had not yet been fulfilled? God told me to live. With all of my strength and the hope that He would provide more strength daily, I determined to hang on until my breakthrough arrived!

During this waiting period in my life, every morning I would wake up between one and two o'clock. The house was dark and still; often, I could feel the spirit of death in the atmosphere. I shared my seven-year-old granddaughter's room with her. I had a hospital bed, commode, and a walker.

When I was awakened in the early morning hours I would get up and go down the hall to the office. I would sometimes stand as long as I could, and at times I would pull a stool to the window and sit for at least an hour looking out at the night sky and praying to the Lord. There were many things I would say as I reflected over my life and the events that led me here.

In the early morning hours there was one song that would come to mind, and I would sing it while sitting by the window "Only Believe":

> Only Believe; only believe.
> All things are possible; only believe.
> Only believe; only believe.
> All things are possible; only believe.
>
> Do you believe? Do you believe?
> All things are possible; do you believe?
> Do you believe? Do you believe?
> All things are possible; do you believe?
>
> Yes, I believe; yes, I believe.
> All things are possible; yes, I believe.
> Yes, I believe; yes, I believe.
> All things are possible; yes, I believe.

There was one other song I would sing the chorus of (because at that time I did not know the lyrics) during the closing of my prayer time and visitation with the Lord, This was my personal variation of the classic hymn:

Jesus, Jesus, how I trust You;
how I've proved You over and over.
Jesus, Jesus, Precious Jesus!
O for grace to trust You more...

I would often tell the Lord, "I know You can do any-thing...I'm not sure if You will have my organs trans-planted, or if You will just come in the room, and by your supernatural power touch me and make my liver and kid-neys brand-new. Whatever your will is, I am confident that You know what is best for me."

Yes, I cried...I cried for me, and I cried for those like me who were waiting for the dawning of a new day in hopes that it brought our deliverance from pain, sickness, and death. It wasn't out of pity, or because my suffering was so great; I wept because I realized that if I held on to my faith in the Omnipotent God, He would show me how great His love was for me.

It is a profound difference when you read the Scriptures and read how Jesus died that we might have a right to eternal life. However, to be in the midst of death and feel safe in Jesus' loving arms, makes the words on the pages come alive in your heart. I cannot die...not now...when He has told me to live!

I wept because in my weakness, in my holding on, God's strength was made perfect. The Holy Spirit revealed to me all of God's thoughts, enveloping love, and plans for me. The Holy Spirit lifted God's Spirit inside of me. This lifting caused strength and the realization that He had commanded me to live and not die. So, no matter how long it takes, I know I have the strength to press into that place of manifestation.

I thank God; He always has a ram in the bush, a witness

of His goodness, grace, and mercy. It testifies of the storms and the pressing that occurs when God is working on one of His children to bring them to the magnificent place He desires them to be in this life.

No one is immune from struggle, difficulties, pain, or even strife, but it's how you perceive and handle it that always makes the difference. My brother in Christ, Pastor Gerald Bess, is one more witness testifying for the Lord. He visited me when I initially got sick in August, and he communicated with me via cell phone and text messages during my trials.

There were many times in those night watches when I would text or call him. Ironically, God always had him available so we could talk about faith. Gerald encouraged me to stand firm, and I assured him that my faith in God was all I had to trust in. It was during one of those many talks with Gerald that God revealed to me He had faith in the faith that He had put inside of me. I realized that God has given every person a measure of faith, and that measure of faith is in direct proportion to the things we will have to deal with in our lives in this Earth realm. Neither you nor I will ever go through anything that our faith is not equipped to bring us through... no matter how grievous or devastating it may be!

I believe God sent Gerald and Shelley to hold my hand in a tangible sense—to speak life in my ear gates daily so that death could not take hold of my thoughts. This allowed my emotions to lay dormant in the midst of circumstances which could cause them to be volatile at any given moment. Indeed, they both spoke life, one in reference to my impending future and the other to my immediate circumstance. Oh hallelujah, God! You covered all the bases, even with the ones who were constantly praying for me.

I believe the midnight hour always comes to the life of the believer. The differences are as vast as the oceans are from the sky. One believes unto life and the other unto death. Some people are dead in their living, and some are living even though they are dying.

I have come to realize that in the darkest moments of our lives, God's movement is spectacular. Look at how He waits patiently when we are still, sometimes exhausted, from trying to do it our own way, lacking strength when everything in our environment is also still. It may feel like hopelessness—without form, void, and dark—upon the vastness of our circumstances. Then God's Spirit moves…yes, He moves upon the darkness and says, "Let there be light." The ray of hope, the light of life dawns, and it is always good.

It is difficult to hear God in the chaos of life, in the day-to-day hustle and bustle, yet when we get still, absorbed by His presence, the understanding of what God is really doing in our lives comes into our view. The midnight is long and difficult when we lack understanding. When we see everything but our faith in the One who holds our very breath of life, it weakens us, and we find ourselves doubting we will ever make it through.

During my midnight hour, the Holy Spirit kept asking me, "Do you trust Me?" My response was always, "Yes, Lord." This, of course, helped my outlook toward the future. I did not focus on the barriers of my present state; I focused on the future me God allowed me to see.

I have found when you come out of the midnight hour, find patience with God, and rest in Him, then and only then does the day break. That abundant life Jesus promised is waiting right there. We must all learn how to endure hardship as good soldiers, knowing that our patience works a far better reward. Indeed, there is a blessing on the other side.

Great is God's faithfulness toward us all because as His dear children we have become benefactors through Christ Jesus. For the joy of it all, He was obedient, even unto death...yes, even for the joy of knowing I would get through the midnight hour. You, my friend, can and will get through too. According to your faith, be it unto you. "Oh death, where is your sting? Oh grave, where is your victory?"

Here are the full lyrics to the song I used to sing in my midnight hour, "'Tis So Sweet to Trust in Jesus." I pray these words bring strength to you as they have often brought to me.

'Tis so sweet to trust in Jesus,
Just to take Him at His word;
Just to rest upon His promise;
Just to know, thus saith the Lord.

Jesus, Jesus, how I trust Him,
How I've proved Him o'er and o'er,
Jesus, Jesus, Precious Jesus!
O for grace to trust Him more.

O how sweet to trust in Jesus,
Just to trust His cleansing blood;
Just in simple faith to plunge me,
'Neath the healing, cleansing flood.

Jesus, Jesus, how I trust Him,
How I've proved Him o'er and o'er,
Jesus, Jesus, Precious Jesus!
O for grace to trust Him more.

Yes, 'tis sweet to trust in Jesus,
Just from sin and self to cease;
Just from Jesus simply taking
Life and rest, and joy, and peace.

Jesus, Jesus, how I trust Him,
How I've proved Him o'er and o'er,
Jesus, Jesus, precious Jesus!
O for grace to trust Him more.

I'm so glad I learned to trust Thee,
Precious Jesus, Savior, Friend;
And I know that Thou art with me,
Wilt be with me to the end.

Jesus, Jesus, how I trust Him,
How I've proved Him o'er and o'er,
Jesus, Jesus, precious Jesus!
O for grace to trust Him more.

Chapter 12

MATURING IN FAITH

*Faith is an established conviction concerning things
unseen and a settled expectation of future reward.*

INHALE; TAKE A deep breath; now exhale. That was done
with little effort on your part...and yet we struggle with
grasping our own faith. Every waking moment of every
single day, whether you are an active participant or not, is
a journey of faith.

Most people don't realize it; however, and they wrestle
with things in this life that have been conquered over 2000
years ago. Jesus took the keys of death and the grave from
Satan's clutches and put boundaries on what he could or
could not do. Jesus overcame the world and all of its devices,
in order that we, the joint heirs, could have abundant life.

Yet there is a struggle to find identity, relationship, and
of course the tangible representation of what we call faith.
What is faith? It is a common denominator, a catalyst that
fuels the very elements of what we possess or do not possess in our lives, but we wrestle with understanding it.

The Book of Hebrews tells us, "Now faith is the substance of things hoped for, the evidence of things not seen"
(Heb. 11:1). Faith is the tangible representation of the very
thing you and I might be hoping for. Faith is what makes
the invisible realm visible, the unseen things seen, the
intangible tangible. Faith is the substance, the elements,
the building blocks, the arresting and possessing of the
things that are already in place by the divine will of God—
literally, bringing what is already existing in the spirit
realm into physical manifestation here on Earth.

Take the greatest asset that you have inside of you, God's Eternal Spirit, and unlock the barriers and harnesses of your life perspective; then soar freely in the knowledge of God's complete ability to bring your heart's desires to pass. Mature faith knows, inherently, that there are no impossibilities in God. Impossibilities come to mind when we put our own psychological barriers in a place where pure faith should reside.

The Word of God tells us that He gives every person a measure of faith, and where there is no knowledge of that measure, there will always be a lack of activation. Circumstances in life cannot give you faith; they can only activate the faith that already resides in you. Most people don't know how much faith they really have until it's been put under the fires of life—when the worst thing happens and somehow they make it through. I have said this before, and I will say it again and again: you must handle your faith in order to realize how much you really possess.

My story is a story of God's deep abiding love for me. He created me in His image and likeness, yet I understand that because the spiritual me is housed in an earthly body, I will have shortcomings and flaws. My story is about His love and grace, which announces to the world: even when it appears that I am in a state of brokenness, I am still complete in Him by His will.

My completeness is in Him alone, and I know it because His grace was transmuted into my faith. I had a double transplant because that was who I was created to be. I never considered transplant as an option; all I knew was God was going to heal me. I began to trust in His Word. Now let me say this: I believe because of my human frailties I was incapable of trusting on my own. However, God's own Spirit inside of me reminded my spirit, which is of God, that I am a daughter of the Most High and that through Christ's unselfish sacrifice of shedding His blood for me, I had a birthright to go back to the throne where I was created and ask my Creator to heal my brokenness.

I believe that when Jesus had His human experience, for a season He did not realize in His natural consciousness that He was the Son of God. He was a babe; He had to grow and mature, until one day He heard His Heavenly Father calling from the inside of His being, and from that point on, He was about His Father's business. Jesus had a mandate on His life, just as we all do. That mandate led Him to the Cross and subsequently to being seated at the right hand of the Father.

He experienced thirty-three years of maturing; thirty-three years of getting acquainted with His faith; thirty-three years preparing to evolve into a faith that led Him to the Cross, knowing that three days later He would be resurrected by the same power that dwelt inside Him. Eternity spoke then, and Eternity speaks now, loudly proclaiming, "My peace I give you, not as the world gives it." The world can only give a counterfeit version of peace—money, cars, houses, job security, fame—but it can't settle your spirit and put you in the presence of the Living God. Peace and tranquility always stand in the realm of faith. By faith the worlds were formed, because when God spoke, He already knew what *the Word* was going to do.

You might say, it is easy for God to have faith in Himself because He created all things. That is precisely why we too should have faith in Him. Remember the exercise at the outset of this chapter: inhale...now exhale. You did not do that for you; you did it because God said you could.

I often tell people that I was born to believe; I am a faith vessel, and so are you. Fundamentally, we all are created the same...on the inside, spiritually. What separates us is not our races, skin color, or sexuality, but our humanism. That's man's way of thinking, not God's. We were never designed to put more emphasis on the creature (man) than the Creator (God). Mature faith understands that it is He who ushers in life and gives mortals their spiritual capabilities. Without the Creator, nothing would exist—and understanding this fundamental truth allows the human being to be whatever the Creator, not the creature, designed it to be. All of us have a need to mature at some point in our natural and spiritual lives. It is only then that we can understand and begin to see our existence and full potential through the eyes of God.

Chapter 13

GOD USES THE HANDS OF A MAN

O N MAY 13, 2014—one year and two months after my transplant surgery—Dr. Hundley and I sat down together to discuss that momentous occasion and compare notes. He began by telling me his powerful personal testimony—the hand of God on his life that had led him to Piedmont Transplant Center just in time to perform my liver transplant surgery.

"I grew up a missionary kid," he told me, "grew up out of the country. My parents were pastors, but I never had any kind of personal faith myself at all, zero." While Dr. Hundley ended up going to a Christian college, he saw himself at this time of his life as the man in John Bunyan's brilliant Christian allegory *Pilgrim's Progress,* who tried to jump over the wall onto the path of Life instead of going through the gate of Salvation. "And that was me. I just jumped onto the path; I'd never gone through the gate...I never had any real faith of my own." Tiring of acting like a Christian when he had no personal faith, Dr. Hundley told his wife, a sincere follower of Jesus, "It should be obvious to you that I don't share this faith with you, but I'm telling you I don't. I don't believe in Jesus."

In 2007, however, Dr. Hundley had a Damascus road experience. He was in his last year of training for transplant surgery, and one Sunday, his sister dragged him to her church: "I slept through the whole sermon...[I] wasn't paying attention at all, thinking everyone there was [an idiot]...thinking about where I was going to take my sister for dinner." But when a woman came up to him at the end of service and asked if she could pray for him, Dr. Hundley acquiesced.

> She put her hand on my shoulder, and she cried out, "Lord, look at this broken vessel!" I grew up Methodist, and things like this don't happen. She basically yelled that, and it was like a wave of God's love fell on me, and I was on the floor. I had been thinking about where to take my sister to dinner, and [next thing I knew] I was on the floor. I stood up a new creature after that... That changed everything for me.

Dr. Hundley then told me the story of how he, unexpectedly, arrived at Piedmont Transplant Center in Atlanta. He had been in medical school from 1996 to 2000, and in training from 2000 to 2008. His first job after his fellowship was in Detroit—and sixteen months later he and his wife moved to what he felt was his dream job in Kentucky. There he became the Director of the liver transplant program, which performed 35 liver transplants a year. Three years into his new job, a friend from Piedmont Transplant Center began calling Dr. Hundley, inviting him to come to Atlanta to interview at the transplant center. Dr. Hundley was not at all interested—he had grown up in Kentucky, he told his friend. He had friends there, and a job he enjoyed. Finally, after his friend called a third time, Dr. Hundley told him honestly, "The only reason I would ever interview with you is to manipulate [the situation]...to get help here in Kentucky, to get another hepatologist."

His friend readily agreed, and to Dr. Hundley's surprise, after one interview in Atlanta, Kentucky immediately gave him everything he'd been asking for during the past three years. He went to Atlanta for a second interview, while waiting for Kentucky's follow-through, and was "blown away all along by how great the team was there...Everybody I met with, I kept thinking 'Oh man, I would love to get this person up to Kentucky; they are so good.' That was my mind-set.'" Nevertheless, Dr. Hundley had difficulty seeing Atlanta as a real possibility for him. He told his wife on the drive home from his second interview, "It's a great job, but it's not home."

When he arrived home in Kentucky, Dr. Hundley did something he had not done before; he prayed about the job in Atlanta. He wanted to be absolutely certain he was making the right decision.

> I prayed, and I asked God to let me wake up with a clear knowledge of what I was supposed to do. I was thinking, *I know it's staying in Kentucky, but let me be 100 percent [sure] because right now I'm only like 95 percent*...I woke up the next day, and as soon as I was awake, I knew that I was supposed to come. Beyond a shadow of a doubt, 100 percent—never had a second thought after that. I told my wife that morning, "This is going to surprise you, but this is like a gift of assurance that this is what we are supposed to do." It has been the best—for me professionally, for my family, my marriage, and friendships. It has been the best year of our twenty years of marriage by far, an unbelievable year in lots and lots of different ways.

Dr. Hundley acknowledged that career-wise it might not have seemed like a smart move—"to go from being the boss of a program" to being the "low man on the totem pole, not in charge of anything." But for him, "It was clear...that's what He wanted me to do, and that's what we've done, and it's been amazing." *1139gold* To me, Dr. Hundley's testimony was evidence of the way God rewards obedience—and of the greater purposes that would touch my own life. "You moved when God said move," I told him, "because He had a plan."

We then began to discuss the actual transplant surgery, which took place on March 8, 2013. Dr. Hundley told me that my "fame" had preceded me: "I had heard about you already. People had said, 'Humungous liver—unbelievable—huge kidneys—all this stuff." Though he had been on call a few times since beginning work at Piedmont, my case was the first liver transplant that came up during his call. He sat in his office looking at my CT Scan, thinking he had never seen a liver that big before. In fact, no one among his colleagues, in their collective 60 years of experience, had seen a liver of that size. He was also anticipating that this was *not* going to be his first liver case at Piedmont though he had done many back in Kentucky: "People can hear that you're good surgically, but it doesn't matter at all until you get to a new place and establish that you are a capable surgeon…I was thinking, *Dr. Johnson is responsible for making sure I'm a good, safe surgeon before he…lets me loose…He's probably going to do this one [himself].*"

Nonetheless, Dr. Hundley came into my room to introduce himself and talk to me the evening before the surgery, and he was immediately struck: "I looked at you and I knew that you were a follower of Jesus. I sensed the Spirit of God in you the moment that I came into the room."

> The last thing I do before I go in is…[pray] as I'm washing my hands, asking God to take over my mind, my hands—to let His hands control my hands…[I] re-center myself on the fact that it's not about me; it's not about my glory; it's about His glory. So the anxiety always leaves me before I start the operation.

But there are some instances, he told me, when he meets people beforehand, and the anxiety is gone immediately: "Right away I know, 'She belongs to Him, and I'm just a hammer that He's swinging. I don't have to worry about this one'—and that's how I felt that day." After introducing himself, Dr. Hundley told me about the prayer line that prays for him and for the patient the moment that he accepts a new surgery, five real prayer warriors that include his wife and sister. I, in turn, told him that I was on a prayer line every day, and they would be praying as well. Then I asked him to take pictures for me and to do one more thing, "You guys just do your job, and God will take care of the rest."

The next morning, Dr Hundley said, as he was washing his hands in preparation to go into the operating room, he could feel the Holy Spirit all over his hands. Dr. Johnson was also in the room—and he wasn't washing his hands. He said to Dr. Hundley, "You got this?" It was the first time Dr. Hundley knew that he would be doing the surgery.

> I was surprised. To be honest with you though, the hardest part of transplant surgery, you didn't have. You didn't have severe portal hypertension, big huge swollen veins all over the place, but you had a problem that nobody else has, which is, you couldn't get to anything because it was so huge. I've done polycystic liver disease transplants before, but never anything like yours.

We then began talking about the nitty-gritty details of my operation. I had read Dr. Hundley's notes before we sat down to talk, and I had a few questions.

Me: . . . I looked at some of your notes, and your notes were saying that somehow the liver had attached itself to my abdomen...you said it left a hole in my abdomen and you had to repair it. When you were in there, what did you do first? [Did you go] to the kidney first?

Dr. Hundley: I mobilized or...split your kidney and your liver away...You have to mobilize it [because] it's attached to your abdominal wall and your back and everything else.

Me: What does "mobilize it" [mean]?

Dr. Hundley: Mobilize just means [to] divide all the attachments of your liver to everything else. I still didn't have room. I could tell that with your kidney there, I wasn't going to be able to have enough room. I'm sure I opted to take your right kidney out [in order] to have room...You always separate the right kidney from the liver...because there are soft tissue and connections there. But your kidney was so big that I just decided...there's no way we were going to leave this kidney in—plus, it had huge cysts. It probably caused that infection that you had before, so I took that out right then. I took the whole kidney out.

Then I had enough room after removing the kidney that I could see underneath the liver. It's hard for me to describe what it felt like. People were making up excuses to come into that operating room that day because it was unbelievable...every time I looked up from the table there were about 12 people against the wall looking like, "Wow, I've never seen anything like that!"

Me: Did you take a break at all?

Dr. Hundley: No.

Dr. Hundley and the team pressed on, and when he had finally put the clamps on my liver and cut it out, he could not believe the size. He picked it up, held it against his chest with both arms, and moved to place it on the table. "That's the picture I wish we had," he told me, "I'm six-foot-six, and it's making me look like a little kid. It was just gigantic." Dr. Hundley is quick to observe,

> The surgery was very, very challenging, but any good liver transplant surgeon could have done it...I know that [the Lord] didn't order me here because technically I'm better than the other surgeons here—because I'm not. They're phenomenal...I *can* tell you this, in 2006 or up until August 26, 2007, *it was all about me.*

The whole process of his medical training, Dr. Hundley told me, was one ambitious goal after another: he was going to get into medical school; once he got in, he determined to be the best medical student there. Then he made it his goal to be one of the six students who received a third-year AOA (honor society induction); and finally, he resolved to graduate summa cum laude...During this time, he was always thinking, "If I achieve this goal, that will bring me joy, peace, and happiness...I wanted to glorify myself...[but ultimately] it did nothing for me."

All these experiences make Dr. Hundley both cautious about not seeking glory for himself, and passionate about giving glory to the only One who is worthy of it. He has discovered that real joy and peace come from "figuring out that it's not about me at all, it's about His glory. Real joy comes from knowing that. As a physician, real joy, honestly, is walking into a room and knowing I don't have to do anything for this patient; God is going to have His way. She's His, and I can just be still and let Him swing that hammer."

He has had so many experiences with patients in the operating room when he has felt God's presence so strong, that he no longer needs any evidence that God moves. One time, he was doing a transplant in Michigan, and a "clamp popped off of the vena cava—the biggest blood vessel in the body. It just fell off, and the amount of bleeding...is hard to describe." The blood loss is so rapid it can mean immediate death. But, as Dr. Hundley notes,

> Almost [as soon as] it was happening, I felt God's Spirit. And immediately I got it stopped before it was even a problem...Every time something like that happens—when I see that He cares enough about you or...this person for Him to do this, it starts getting through my thick skull that He cares that much about me too. Slowly, but surely, the scales begin to fall off my eyes every day. [I'm learning to live] from an internal perspective.

That internal perspective refers to the person you really are, the calling that is uniquely yours. The "true you" lives and matures and partners with the Lord in His purposes for your life. One of the reasons I called this chapter "God Uses the Hands of Man" is because that is what God needed. He wanted Dr. Hundley's hands, and He came upon them so strongly that this humble man of God could feel the presence of the Holy Spirit all over them. In our conversation, Dr. Hundley observed that it is rare, even in the Old Testament, for the Lord to just *do* something; He often wants to partner in some way with men and women: "[The Lord] almost always chose to say [to the Israelites, for instance], 'Go walk around Jericho"...or to Moses, "Hold the staff up out here"—and it didn't have anything to do with Moses being any smarter or stronger; it was just [the fact that he was] a willing vessel." It's the greatest accolade—to be a willing vessel. How interesting, then, that the lady who prayed for Dr. Hundley years before had cried out, "Lord, look at this broken vessel!" That transforming moment, and all the choices Dr. Hundley has made since— to walk in obedience, to allow the Lord to circumcise his heart, to become a willing vessel—has led to this beautiful purpose, as the Lord uses him to help heal other broken vessels. It brings the Lord so much glory!

How I have wanted the world to see how the Lord has kept me in these last 17 years! While the cysts in my liver were metastasizing, so were the cysts on my kidneys. My liver got up to 26 pounds and had shifted some of my internal organs. When I first saw the photographs of what they took out of me, it was two weeks after surgery. I wept— because only God could have kept me. God was with me all the way; I only stayed on the transplant list 50 days! Fifty is the number of Jubilee. So I celebrate the Lord and my life in Him. I really wanted the world to see what God has done for me! (Please note: the following photographs are graphic.)

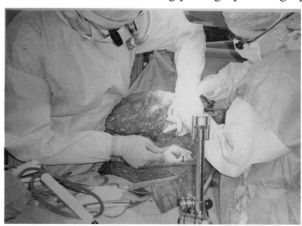

On the operating table while Dr. Hundley works to disconnect my native liver for removal.

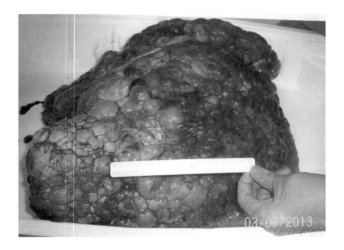

The ruler in the above photograph indicates the size of a normal liver. When I was initially diagnosed in 1996, the cysts were inside the liver. As you can see, by 2013, they totally consumed it. Remember, I had no pain at all until I got sick on August 14, 2012.

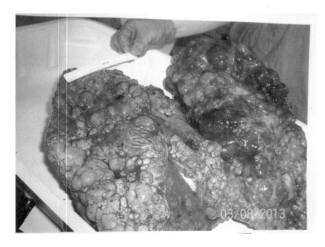

When Dr. Hundley turned my liver over, it just fell open on the table. As you can see, it is totally covered inside and out with cysts. You would probably agree with me that God is a keeper, and that He does have a plan in place for my life!

Sometimes a picture is worth a thousand words. I know there are a few reading this book who are questioning their faith. I pray that each of you will stir up your faith today: faith in God was all I had when no one else could help me. My life has continuously played out before others so that, when His divinity touched it so wonderfully, all would see His handprint and say, "It is the Lord's doing, and it is marvelous in our sight."

I made it, with God's help—*and you can too!*

Chapter 14

MOUNTAIN-HIGH FAITH

Mountain-high faith allows the supernatural you to do what you were created to do. It forces the natural you to become subservient and yield to the power of Christ within you.

I N THE LAST half century I have experienced many things, both good and bad, yet I have come to realize that all those experiences were instrumental in the development of my faith. Most people never realize the magnitude of the level of faith that they have. Many of their creative gifts of God lay dormant because the recipient of this gift never realizes its full potential.

Let me ask you, what good is knowing how to play the piano if you never play it? What good is your gift if you never hear or even develop an appreciation for the beautiful melodies that can be created, simply at the stroke of your own hand?

I believe we as humans get so swallowed up in our own humanity that we never discover the beauty and power behind our deity—that God part of us that allows us to soar beyond the confinements of these earthly bodies into a dimension that has no limitations, no spiritual boundaries, but totally embraces the harmony of the Deity's presence interwoven in our very own existence.

You may ask, "How do you know this? How can this be possible?" I know this because in the grander scheme of the ever-present mind of God is His faith—and in that faith is His faithfulness to our faith. He placed this faith inside each of us during our creation by His manifold wisdom.

We must come to understand that before we were, faith is and shall always be. To be created in God's image is to possess His divine attributes, yet to truly see the attributes of God is to look through the eyes of faith. Faith says, we must first believe that God is, and that He is a rewarder of those that diligently seek Him (see Heb. 11:6). How can you diligently seek Him without a heart that sees beyond the visible, into the invisible, by faith?

Mountain-high faith declares that faith is always in the commanding position—a position of authority, a standing order that governs everything that you do in accordance with the divine will of God, based on the creative design that He has for your life.

Faith is the most influential part of your life. It is the driving force behind your dreams, aspirations, and belief system, sustained by the power of God Himself.

Faith is the canvas for a heart of obedience to God, regardless of public opinion or the ridicule of family and friends. Faith in the infallible, immutable, and eternal Word of God and the internal workings of our soul, acquiesces with the universe that God will not fail me. He will not abandon me, or leave me without answers or a way of escape.

Faith is knowing that the mind power of God regulates all things that exist, and yet nothing regulates Him. If He knows the ant by name, then I can rest assured He is intimately aware of what is going on within the physiological, psychological, sociological, spiritual, environmental, and economical realms of my life. So then my resolve becomes, God will work the needed miracle if I dare to stand on His Word.

Why then are most people afraid to believe? They lack knowledge about the Holy Spirit who dwells inside of them, navigating them through the obstacle course of life;

knowledge about Jesus, the Son of God, who through His selfless sacrifice paid the ransom of His life in order that we all might be eternally free from the bondages of sin, sickness, death, and the grave; knowledge about God's great love for us as His children, like any other Father, who desires only the best for His children.

Many things happen in the lives of God's people, and some are so very tragic that they harden the hearts of the people. In my own tragedies, I did not get angry and turn from God, but I realized the hopeless state I was in, and I ran...no, I crawled to the only true power that could help me. Do you know, the first thing He did was pick me up and made me stand on my feet; He told me, "I am not going to carry you. You must walk this out; your strength lies in you understanding all that I have put inside of you." It was at this point that I realized I indeed had much to learn.

Through His grace and a myriad of circumstances, God has convinced me that He is the real deal. There is nothing counterfeit or fabricated about His existence or His ways. Much of it is outlined in the Bible, and I will be the first to admit, I have experienced God in ways I never could have imagined, even though there are many things revealed in His Word.

The truth is, He is always revealing His ways, because He is living and He is much larger than all of His creations. Trusting in Him is the first step to understanding Him. Yet, no trust is validated without the anchor of faith.

Faith is the tangible representation of all things, seen and unseen. Faith sees it before the manifestation ever enters the earthly realm. Man says seeing is believing; however, God says, through faith, believing is seeing.

Let me pose this question to you: If you were dying, would you rather hold on to what you are seeing, or trust in the God that created you who you cannot see? Be honest…most people choose the former over the latter, and they die in unbelief.

I was praying once for a young lady who had breast cancer; through chemo and radiation they eradicated the cancer, yet they encouraged her to get a mastectomy as a precaution, in case of recurrence. When her mother called and asked me to pray, I told her I would. By faith I went to God in prayer; I was still recovering from transplant surgery. When I asked him to completely heal the young lady, God said to me, "I already have." He then said, "I am a perpetual healer, daughter; I always heal. The problem is, people don't believe, and they die in unbelief." I called the young lady's mother a few days later and told her what the Lord had said to me. At the time I was talking to her God revealed to me that her daughter's faith was not strong to trust God for what He had already done, and that she would have the mastectomy. Two weeks later her daughter had the mastectomy. All I know is what I heard the Lord say.

Oh ye of little faith. It is hard to get around our environmental influences, to look beyond what we see and what our emotions dictate. Yet God is not moved by our emotions; He is moved by our faith. Faith is not some whimsical fantasy, something made up in our human minds. It is a state of being in unison with the mind of God.

Faith is a gift from God, just like the indwelling of His Spirit. The Spirit understands your faith and always directs you toward it. Remember, we are saved by grace, yet that grace can only be acknowledged by our faith. Faith is a necessary nutrient to our soul's existence just like air is necessary to our bodies.

Long before I ever saw my healing in the natural, I saw myself healed in the spirit. Whenever I would have dreams of myself, my abdomen was never enlarged; it was always as it had been before my diagnosis. I could see beyond the impossibilities into the realm of possibilities, because I was looking not to man or myself, but I had my eyes on the God who could and would heal me.

Once I understood that there were no failures in God and that His Word indicated that He had healed me, I held on to that. You see, faith is not a fad or cliché; faith is a conscious decision to release all doubt and believe—not in what God will do, but what He has already done.

It takes work, discipline, and recalibration of the thought processes because we are so accustomed to believing only in what we can see. Yet the simple truth is that everything you see around you was created in the invisible realm— the stars, moon, sun, trees, birds, oceans, and all of creation. Faith can move the metaphorical mountains in our lives, because faith trusts in the God who by faith created the physical mountains we see every day.

No matter what we can imagine, God can create something much bigger...exceeding abundantly above all we can ask or think. What I am trying to get you to understand is, why worry, when worry changes absolutely nothing? Why not put all of your cares in the Creator's capable hands. God knows the plans He has for our lives and with each plan there is an expected end for us to get to. There is a plan because this journey is not a journey of chance. God already knows our every reaction, thought, deed, and doubt. He has made provision for them all. Remember, He knew you long before you knew what you knew about yourself.

Run until you're exhausted; then run some more, and you will ultimately discover as I have that there is no escaping the omnipresence of God. My friend, faith doesn't run from God; it runs to God.

Let me share with you a few things I have learned about the gift of faith and its supernatural attributes.

Faith is the supernatural ability to believe God without doubt.

Faith is the supernatural ability to combat unbelief.

Faith is the supernatural ability to meet adverse circumstances with confidence.

Faith is trust in God's message and words.

Faith is an inner conviction provoked by an urgent and higher calling.

Faith is an established conviction concerning things unseen and a settled expectation of future reward.

Faith is substance, a real or essential part of anything.

Faith is because God is.

Faith is an essential tool in this life.

Faith lives in a position of authority, with the intent to command.

Faith is in the possession of every human being.

God is the Author and Finisher of the faith you possess. How much faith you have determines the measure you have to operate in. For instance, when God said, "Let there be light," 186,000 miles per second later, light was.

The very intent of God at that *kairos* (opportune) moment was to create light, and the result was light. God saw the light, that it was good. The same power behind these very words He has given to us, who are created in the likeness of the Godhead (Father, Son, and Holy Spirit).

God tells us in His Word that we can have what we say; however, many of us only speak what we currently have. For example, you say, "I am broke." The result is that you see only lack, no increase. You must condition your heart to believe the Word of God, then your mind and mouth must follow suit. When unity occurs within the heart, you can command whatever you speak, and it will come to pass. Command the needed resources to come. God will work the miracle if you dare stand by faith upon His Word. God's Word and His Laws are immutable (they do not change). His methods, miracles, and manifestations are eternally limitless. Conversely, if God our Redeemer says in His Word that you and I have faith, then you and I have faith.

Ask God to give you the grace to use the faith that you have.

Let's compare for a moment faith and hope. Faith is a *conviction* in the heart that says it will happen; it has an *expectation* that it will happen. Hope, on the other hand, is a *feeling* in the mind that what is wanted will happen. Now you have a desire accompanied by an expectation. They both carry an expectation, but faith has nothing to do with your feelings. Faith is an inner knowing that He can and will do it, an unwavering trust in God. Commitment in believing allows the impossible to become possible. Mountain-high faith always believes.

Chapter 15

THE SPIRIT-FILLED LIFE

A Spirit-filled life is a relationship with Jesus where the divine and the human give themselves completely to one another.

A SPIRIT-FILLED LIFE IS exactly that. It is a life that has been opened to the incredible possibilities of the Spirit of the Living God revealed completely in the hearts and minds of people. It is not some religious summation to mystical events or a creative allegory with contrived lessons; it is what we were created to possess. A Spirit-filled life is the sum total of what our lives as vessels of God are supposed to resemble.

The real burning question is, how do we arrive at this place and how do we truly identify with it once we have arrived? The Bible says, "Walk in the Spirit, and you won't fulfill the lust of the flesh" (see Gal. 5:16). I have found that the flesh is never satisfied it is always hungering for more. More food, more gratification, more drugs, more alcohol. Depending on your individual vices, these are the things that the flesh continuously desires. However, as children of the light we must mortify this flesh daily and deny it the desires that it craves outside of the will of God.

It takes quite a bit of maturing to get to the place where you become free of the bondage of condemnation in your own mind. You must sever the tie to the old, sinful, body that you have been chained to for years and be free to embrace goodness and the riches of an abundant life in Christ Jesus.

To live a Spirit-filled life is to live a life truly *in* Christ. We are not outside of Him like strangers without any knowledge of His personality or His ways; we have the intimacy of knowing the very essence of God's love, which is personified in Christ and manifested in each believer by the power of His amazing grace at work in our lives.

Initially, when we begin to walk by the Spirit, the Spirit literally lays a path out for us to follow every day. As we continuously follow that path, we learn how to follow God implicitly. We then start to not only walk *on* the path, but also *in unison* with the Spirit as one. We learn how to live a life in the Spirit continuously.

By faith we learn to yield to the Spirit's tugging at our hearts, which reveals to us the path to walk each day, ultimately leading to our spiritual maturation. Of course, it is a process; sometimes the process takes years, but it is worth every bit of it. To knowingly engage the Creator of all things and see the divine plan unfold for one's life is truly fascinating. Best of all is to come to the realization that your entire life has been an incredible journey orchestrated by the triune God Himself; you see the beauty of His plan to perfect your life and experiences so that you not only find God in the process, but yourself as well.

I can't begin to tell you how many times I have been asked about this process that every human being goes through while they are here in this earthly realm. For God, I would imagine the process is simple; however, for those of us who are sometimes unwilling participants in the process, it can take many twists and turns before the greatest truth is revealed in us. The greater the process, the greater the truth.

What truth is this? Our identity—who you and I were created to be in Christ Jesus. The master plan of God is to reconcile His children to Himself, revealed in Christ's life, death, and love for all of us. Why were we sent from heaven in the first place? To experience the fullness of God—the variegated, multifaceted, many-colored, manifold wisdom of God; His character; and all of His glory. "How?" you may ask. By getting deeply acquainted with His love wrapped in flesh, Jesus, and by experiencing the pouring out of that love in our lives during our human experience.

Every human experience is different because every spirit is different. What makes the experiences come alive are the choices each of us makes, whether they are in accordance or not with God's divine will. We may hit-or-miss continually in our attempts to find the perfect fit; however, the truth of who we are is already inside of us, and all we really have to do is get in tune with the voice crying out in the wilderness of the chambers of our own souls. The problem is that no one wants to hear the voice on the inside because it's far more captivating to hear from everything that surrounds us. Can I tell you something seriously? Those outside influences are not all they are made out to be.

There are billions among us who suffer from identity crisis. Not because they haven't found the perfect role to play, but because the role they chose was not the role that they were created for. Understanding this is key: long before God created each of us as spirit beings, He had the purpose for our creation already in His mind. In the mind of God, purpose for the creation existed long before the created thing was. Remember, there are no *oops!* in God, no errors, no misconceptions, no deviations. Just the mind of God in total perfection! God's wisdom is infallible, and His creations always have an explicit purpose.

When a person is told that he or she is nothing, there is nothing further from the truth. It's really incomprehensible in view of God's preeminent wisdom because God has never made any junk: "All things were created by him, and for him" (Col. 1:16).

Chapter 16

LESSONS LEARNED

W HILE PONDERING ON how this book should con-
clude, I began to reflect on my journey and a myriad
of things I have learned, especially about faith and
being tested in adversity. It then occurred to me to leave
some golden nuggets of wisdom for the reader.

1. Faith works. Faith is a gift from God. It's so
   personal that every human being gets his or
   her own portion (Rom. 12:3).

2. Your measure of faith is in direct correlation
   to who you were created to be and what you
   the creation will go through during your
   time here on Earth.

3. Faith is what provokes God to move in our
   circumstances, not our tears and not our
   pleas.

4. You cannot will yourself to believe; it is an
   impartation from God. When God breathed
   into Adam's nostrils and he became a living
   soul, faith became alive in him as well.

5. Just because we do not utilize our faith,
   does not negate the truth that faith resides
   within us.

6. Faith in us becomes real to us when
   we agree in our hearts and mind
   with the Creator's design of that faith.
   Acknowledging your faith makes your faith

usable, and maturing spiritually allows you to understand the depths of that faith.

7. Your faith is designed to believe every word of God, and when you believe, that is when you see it manifested tangibly in your life.

8. God is a healer; it doesn't matter which method He uses. He does have a myriad of options: a doctor, for instance, coming into your room in the midnight hour, or a preacher laying hands on the sick in a prayer line, and the list goes on. The truth is, they could have given me a million livers, and if God had said, "None of them will work. I will bring her home with Me," the result would have been the same. I am healed. Hallelujah, I am healed!

9. God left me in the Earth to tell my story so He could get all of the glory!

10. So many lessons are learned when you can walk a mile in someone else's shoes. You can only pour out to anyone from what you yourself have within.

11. The testing of our faith: If we never go through anything, how will we know what we can or cannot bear? True faith is always tried by fire!

12. Many say, "I wish I had your faith." I will admit that sometimes I wish I could give it away, because some just can't find their way to that level of trust in God. It hurts to pray

with all of your faith with an unbeliever because it's like putting a positive to a negative; there is conflict in our spirits. And how can two walk together except they agree? (See Amos 3:3.) When there is a double standard involved, there is double-mindedness. The Bible tells us, a double-minded man is unstable in all of His ways and should not expect anything from God (see James 1:6–8).

13. A picture is worth a thousand words. Some people need to see it before they will believe it. Yet the truth is, that is not faith. Faith sees far beyond what the natural eyes can see. Faith goes into realms of the unseen. God is a Spirit, and He works His miraculous wonders in the unseen realm or the spirit realm, yet it manifests or materializes in the natural so we can partake in it. Long before I ever entertained the thought of transplant as a option, I saw myself, even in my dreams, always healed, without an extended abdomen. The pictures are to bring to the surface the consciousness of those who live outside of faith. Do you really believe *all* things are possible to those who believe?

I believe that someone this very moment is reading this book who is dealing with a physical affliction; your condition may or may not be as bad as mine was, but I want you to know—the final authority concerning your life is not what the doctors have diagnosed. God always has the last say. Could this be your moment of triumph where you finally realize, "I just need to trust God"? He loves you and desires that you walk in healing. Why would you continue to deny your own birthright from God to live? Settle it today: what do you believe? If you believe God, then you tell yourself what God has already said, "I am the Lord that healeth thee" (Exod. 15:26).

The prophet Isaiah prophesied 800 years before Jesus walked the Earth as a man that "He was wounded for our transgressions, He was bruised for our iniquities: the chastisement of our peace was upon him; and with His stripes *we are* healed" (Isa. 53:5, my emphasis). Jesus' atoning work on the cross, His suffering for physical afflictions—cancer, AIDS, diabetes, heart problems, blindness, the inability to walk or talk, polycystic kidney and liver disease—all of it was nailed to the cross. When Jesus said, "It is finished," that is exactly what He meant in so many ways. Even our eternal resting place was covered by the Cross. Jesus did the hard part; all we have to do is *believe Him!*

Now tell your sickness today: I believe God; Jesus has freed me from sickness; *I am healed in the name of Jesus!* Now, my friend, get up out of your bed and walk in the *name of Jesus!*

We are living in a time right now when God is pouring out miracles. What's stopping you from drinking from His fountain of life? There is no one standing there between God and you, but you.

Let me share with you the story of blind Bartimaeus (which you can read it in its entirety in Mark 10:46–52). As Jesus and His disciples, together with a large crowd, were leaving the city, a blind man named Bartimaeus was sitting by the roadside begging. When he heard that Jesus of Nazareth was passing by, he began to shout, "Jesus, Son of David, have mercy on me!" Many rebuked him and told him to be quiet, but he shouted even louder, "Son of David, have mercy on me!" Jesus stopped and told them to call him. So they called the blind man and told him to get up and cheer up because Jesus was calling him. Throwing his garment aside, he jumped up and came to Jesus. "What do you want Me to do for you?" Jesus asked him. Then the blind man said, "Lord, I want to see." And Jesus said to him, "Go, your faith has healed you." Immediately, he received his sight and followed Jesus along the road.

Look at this faith. The blind man heard that Jesus, the Son of the Living God, was coming and cried out for mercy from the healer. Blind Bartimaeus encounters Jesus just prior to the Cross. The prophesied Messiah is passing by, so faith cries out to the substance, the tangible representation of his faith, "Have mercy on me!" Not even the crowd could deter or silence him: "Son of David, have mercy on me." Notice what he does the moment Jesus calls him. The garment or cloak he was wearing identified him to men as a person who was blind, but when Jesus called him, the second thing faith did was to throw off that old identification, that old life of blindness and despair, because his faith had God's attention. Even though at that present moment he could not physically see, his faith allowed him to see all that was necessary. When Jesus asked him, "What can I do for you?" He was asking him, "What can I do for your faith?" The blind man replied, "Lord, I want to see." Even if no one else is able to open these eyes, I know You can because You made these eyes. Immediately, faith ushered him into his sight. He received his miracle, and he didn't turn back to his old life, but followed Jesus along the road He was traveling.

My friend, I encourage you to step out of those old clothes of sickness and receive by faith what God has for you. This book is just a token, a symbol that right now in your life, no matter the circumstances, or how you got there, He is asking your faith, "What can I do for you?"

I know that took a minute, but I must be obedient to what the Holy Spirit is telling me. Shall we continue with the lessons I have learned?

14. There are no *oops!* in God. God does not make mistakes. His creative authority is so meticulous that He knows the design and purpose of everything He has ever created. We may get confused about what He has created—but He never gets confused. Just consider for a moment the mind power of God: He knows every person who was ever created, their names, shapes, eyes, hair, and skin color; their birthdays and death appointments—even how they will enter into those appointments. God knew the first person you would fall in love with and the first person who would break your heart. He even knows every person who will come in and out of your life. He knows all of our secrets; He has already been in our skeleton closet. God knows what you and I will do, even before we do. Yes, you get to make choices, but He already knows the choices you and I will make. That, my friend, is why Jesus gave us an incredible gift by the Cross; it's called grace, and it covers us every time our humanity falls short of His will. This brings me to my next lesson learned.

15. God always has a perfect plan. When I left home at 17 to go into the military, I never

dreamed I would complete 20 years of service—nor could I have imagined being diagnosed with such an incredibly consuming disease.

After spending years of training and service periodically at various duty stations in Georgia, I vowed I would never live in Georgia, but God had a plan. I would subsequently retire in the very place where it would be necessary, sometime later, for me to have a transplant. Coincidence? Hardly. Let's call it destiny—a perfect plan from a perfect mind. Thank God for His consistency in our lives. Before I was born, before I left Fort Lauderdale, before I was ever diagnosed, before I was transferred to Atlanta, before I retired, before my liver got up to 26 pounds, before the transplant, God had a *perfect plan.*

16. Second chances: I thought initially that would be an appropriate title for this book, but I changed my mind after realizing that while the transplant gave me physical life again, which brought about more opportunities to get things right in life in relationship with God, my true second chance was given over two thousand years before my arrival in the Earth, by Jesus and His sacrifice on the Cross. The resurrecting power that flowed through His mortal body brought healing to the masses. The very same power that led Him to the Cross and to the grave resurrected Him again, and He was seen

forty days after His crucifixion, alive and doing the will of the Father.

For me Jesus spent six hours one Friday on the Cross so I could have the privilege of spending eight hours under His watchful eye, being resurrected from death by receiving a new liver and kidney. The number six represents man...six hours on the Cross for man. The number eight represents new beginnings...eight hours on the operating table for new beginnings. Again, I say there are no *oops!* in God; we get many more chances because of His grace.

17. Wisdom: Wisdom is just as variegated as God is, and it can show up anywhere, even in a storm.

18. Self awareness: True self awareness is our knowledge of the awesome power of God that dwells inside each of us. Outside of Him, you and I cannot even exist. Self-awareness is achieved when we realize our true identities are inextricably linked to our created purpose, and anything outside of that is mere role-play.

19. Presence versus presents: The presence of the great people God has allowed to venture into my life has yielded so much knowledge and fruit to me. Some of them may never know how much joy and life they have extended to me—not from the gifts that they bring. Those things corrode and pass away. True presence, however, will speak in the Earth long after

their mortal voices have become silent. For the presence I am truly grateful.

20. Patience works. There is always a set time with God. He thinks and moves in an orderly and concise manner. Even now, with all I have learned, every now and then I find myself moving ahead of God. Since I have matured a lot in Christ over the years, I usually don't get too far ahead because my spirit begins to feel uncomfortable, and I have to feel connected to God at all times. Even though we might know what to do, the season or the timing it should be done in makes all the difference. We all must learn how to be led by the Spirit; even Jesus followed the leading of the Spirit of God. My friend, patience in God does have its rewards.

21. Prodigal thinking: Now I know I don't have to live a life of condemnation, shame, or guilt, because no matter how great my faults or how egregious my sins may be, God's love and grace toward me is much greater than any of these. I can go to Him, ask for forgiveness, be restored in our relationship, and be made whole.

22. Healing comes from the heart of God. Set your affections and faith there, in pursuit of *your place* of purpose, *your place* of creation, *your place* of refuge, in the pureness of His heart.

23. Keep an open mind when it comes to *God*.
He can be full of surprises when you limit
Him in your mind. When my former
internal medicine doctor came into my
room during his rounds when I was initially
hospitalized, he reminded me of the advice
he had given me years before about my liver:
"Never let anyone cut your liver unless I tell
you it is okay." He came by to let me know
it was time for something to be done, ie., a
transplant. When he left, I turned my face
to the wall, and I asked the Lord, "Is this
Your will for me to have transplant surgery?" I began to weep when it was settled
in my spirit. I realized someone would have
to die in order for me to live. I then acquiesced: "Not my will, but Thy will be done."
Limiting God in our heart and mind makes
it difficult for us, not for God.

24. What about Me? It's funny how we can let
the external things in our lives dictate our
responses, our emotions, and even manipulate what faith we have. So many times we
have displaced our faith. We put it in people,
and they hurt and disappoint us. We put it
in our social status, jobs, and bank accounts.
Isn't it amazing that, when the bottom falls
out around us, some of us run to God and
ask, "What are You doing to my life? I didn't
ask for this. What about my needs, my
desires, my happiness? What about me?"
Sometimes our cry is *so* great, *so* loud and

agonizing we can't hear Him saying to us,
"What about Me? Have you really forgotten
the Me that is inside of you? I am and I
will always be the greatest part of you. Now
come let us (you and Me) reason together;
I'm sure we will come up with a solution.
After all, I created you, and I know the plans
I have for you."

From my early teens, I've always known there was so much more to God than I would hear about in my home church. There were many things in my life that took up space because I was trying to understand life and how I fit into it. My journey has had a lot of twist and turns, which fuels my life's quest. I will continue to love, embrace, and explore every aspect of God that He reveals to me, and by faith, I will continue to allow Him to use my life however He desires. Yes, I believe that all things in God are possible, from healing to raising the dead. My God has proven to me, He can do anything but fail. My friend, find your place in God and live much more abundantly...According to *your faith,* be healed.

I love you,

—Dr. Dee

Dear Reader, here's a golden nugget for you... There is a special code inside of this book. This code gives you access to my personal vault on my website. For a limited time, that vault can be opened with that access code, and there is a golden opportunity that will bless you waiting inside.

Chapter 17

WHAT ABOUT ME?

*These three little words have such profound depth. Then
again, it depends on who's asking the question…*

I REALLY DESIRED TO share with you about the last 17
years of my life. Some of you might say that I've been
through more in 17 years than you've been through in
your entire life—but this is just a snapshot, a glimpse to let
you see that with God, we are truly overcomers.

We so often seem to focus on just what is happening
in our small section of the world. We set out trying to
achieve and please, yet more often than not, when we get
to the top of our proverbial mountain, there is little if any
applause at all. Everyone else is too busy scaling their own
mountains. Along the way we fall, have disappointments,
and even shattered dreams or aspirations. We label ourselves based on the world's standards for success, and deep
inside there is always something missing.

Success outside of our divine purpose is not really success at all. It's like taking credit for someone else's invention,
or taking someone's marathon trophy and putting your
name on it, when the truth is you can barely walk a mile.

We deceive ourselves a lot because we feel the pressure of
these standards. How many humans have committed sui-
cide, when their alter persona, which was created outside of
their purpose felt so displaced that depression set in like a
deep, swallowing hold, tightening its grip on every side daily,
as they went out into the world? Often, our own human
frailties get the best of us because they choke our God-given
purpose and substitute what the world places value on.

We were never created to please others; instead, each of us must find the truth of who we are and apply our God-given talents fervently toward the mandate that was set from God's own creative authority. Each one of us was designed with a specific purpose in mind, yet we get so sidetracked with the noises of our external environment we can't hear God speaking in His still, quiet voice.

Do you realize that if we all channeled our own energies, gifts, talents, and purposes individually, yet in poetic harmony with everyone else in their creative space, what a symphony of pure love we would create? I believe in the human spirit because I believe there is goodness in everyone; after all, we are created in God's own image. However, when goodness is unfamiliar with its own identity and comes face to face with evil, it will inherently take on the form of that with which it identifies most. Evil is in the world because the prince of darkness is in the world, but the force of good inside of us all is greater, if we could just see each other as God does.

Let's go back for a minute to discuss each of us working in harmony with others who have discovered the value of their own divine nature. This could cause a great universal work, and we all could collectively end world hunger, poverty, hatred, murder, and wars. We all are inextricably linked together, and whether we agree or disagree, we are our brothers' keeper. Some of us think we are an island to ourselves, yet the more we receive, the more we are supposed to give.

The impoverished among us are not poor because they don't have food or shelter; they're poor because we as a collective choose to abandon them, because of the choices they made or did not make. How many times have you or I made choices that cost us so much and nobody ever knew about it? Sometimes the world makes the choices for you, and you have to live with the consequences.

My story, like your story, has less to do with me and more to do with the divine Creator. What we are or what we are not reflects our choices, which are relevant to our creation. You and I were never created to be self-absorbed or self-loathing; we were created to be magnificent creatures ruling in the Earth.

Sadly, just like Adam and Eve, we let our environmental influences get the best of us. Once we put ourselves in a place in life where we hear outside influences more than the internal voice of truth, we ultimately follow the lie that leads to darkness, and that darkness will always lead to sin, sickness, and death. We are spiritually bankrupt when we have no clue of what is intrinsically inside of us. The strength of our character comes from the power of the Most High who dwells inside of us. The character to respond to any type of adversity, especially sickness, can only be garnered when we understand what we have to work with.

I felt pain, especially when I left the hospital with 56 staples in my abdomen and during that long first night at home when the pain medication did not work. I walked and prayed all night long. The pain did not subside until I started reflecting on something greater than myself.

I imagined Christ on the cross for those six hours one Friday; it just happened to be a Friday for me as well. When I saw His suffering and considered that it made a way for me to live, my resolve became clear to me. Even though I was in pain, all that I had gone through during those 17 years, including my mother's death, was a light affliction.

I can imagine you asking, "Would you do it all again?" My answer would be a resounding yes, because I know it was who I was created to be. Trials come to test our faith.

The greater the faith, the greater the trial. Faith that is not tried is not faith at all.

By the world's standards, I've lost a great deal, but all that I have lost could never compare to what I have, ever-present, to hold onto. My friends, you can get through anything, when your heart and mind line up with all that God has invested in you.

You know, it's okay to get tired sometimes; you do have human attributes. But don't ever let your situation beat you down to the point that you get weary in your spirit. How do you combat weariness when you've been battling sickness for so long? Recalibrate your thoughts; renew your mind daily with the Word of God. You must establish firmly your relationship with Him. Be committed, just as He is committed to you.

The question "What about Me?" really is reciprocal by design. If you focus on Him, He is focused on you. If you give Him praise and glory with your life, He will bless your life. If you hide His Word by faith in your heart, "I'm the Lord God that healeth thee", He will come and heal you. So when you're asking Him, "What about me?" the reciprocal question He is asking you is, "What about Me?"

Chapter 18
A WORD FROM THE LORD

M Y CHILD, YOU hurt, you long, you are misguided, and you look for love in all the wrong places. In the midst of your trials, you cry out, "What About Me?" I always hear your cries, and I ask you today, "What about Me, inside of you?"

I have made you a vessel of Me, so that where there is hatred, you can bring love; where there is wrong, you can bring the spirit of forgiveness; where there is confusion, you can bring harmony; where there is error, you can bring correction and truth; where there is doubt, you can bring faith; where there is sickness, you can bring healing; where there is brokenness, you can be a repairer of the breach; where there is despair, you can bring hope; where there is darkness, you can bring light; where there is sadness, you can bring joy, and where there is loneliness, you can bring Me.

Being a reflection of Me, you must always, seek to give comfort, rather than to be comforted; to understand, rather than to be understood; to love, rather than to be loved; to give rather than to receive. It is by forgetting *self* that you find *yourself* in Me. Remember, it is by forgiving that you are forgiven, and it is by the death of the old man, that you awaken to eternal life.

I have said to you from the depths of My eternal love for you, I always see the best in you, even when you cannot see the best in yourself. That is because you are looking from the outside, and I already know what is on the inside, a replica of *Me!* Healing is always resident inside of you because I am inside of you; you just have to believe.

Chapter 19

MY PRAISE

T HANK YOU FOR using my life, Lord. You are everything to me!

GOD, YOU ARE

You are the air that I breathe

You are the essence of my life

You are the lifter of my head

You are the keeper of my soul

You are my way out

You are my deliverer

You are my restorer

You are God the breaker

You are the Alpha and Omega

You are the beginning and the end

You are the first and the last

You are Jehovah Jireh

You are Jehovah Nissi

You are Jehovah Mekadesh

You are Jehovah Shammah

You are the Prince of Peace

You are the Great I Am

You are Elohim

You are Emmanuel, God with us

You are Adonai

You are El-Elyon

You are Jehovah Rafa

You are the high and mighty one

You are King of kings

You are Lord of lords

You are my shepherd

You are the restorer of the breach

You are the bridge over troubled water

You are my friend

You stick closer than a brother

You are my judge

You are my vindicator

You are my counselor

You are my guide

You are the author, finisher, and perfecter of my faith

You are my Abba

You are my truth

You are my peace

You are my joy

You are the life-giving Spirit

You are the Lord, mighty in battle

You are my fortress

You are an ever-present help in a time of trouble

You are my shield and buckler

You are my sanctuary

You are the rock that is higher than I

You are the great High Priest

You are the balm of Gilead

You are captain of our salvation

You are the many-breasted one

You are merciful

You are kind

You are patient

You are long suffering

You are meek

You are gentle

You are goodness

You are love

You are joy unspeakable

You are a way maker

You are a strong tower

You hung the moon

You hung the stars in the sky

You are the wind that blows

You are my hiding place

You are my secret pavilion

You are the song in my heart

You are my hope for tomorrow

You are the Spirit in me, that part that can never die

You made me in Your image and likeness

You told me to have dominion over the works of
Your hand

You gave me power to tread over serpents and
scorpions and over all the power of the enemy

You told me that no weapon formed against me
shall prosper

You told me that You would deliver me from every
evil work

You told me that I was more than a conquerer
through Christ Jesus

You told me if I ask, I would receive

You said if I seek, I shall find

You said if I knock, it would be opened unto me

You said if I would cry out, You would answer,
"Here am I"

You said You would never leave me or forsake Me
(Heb. 13:5)

You said in Your word that You would not forget
me (Isa. 49:15)

You said You have inscribed my name on the palms
of Your hands and that I am continually
before You (Isa. 49:16)

Oh, You are all together lovely

You are so very kind

You are holy

You are sovereign

You are omnipotent

You are omniscient

You are omnipresent

You are pure

You are righteous

You are faithful

You are the word of life

You are the I am that I am

You are the immutable God

You are Lord God Almighty; which was, and is,
and is to come

You are from everlasting to everlasting

You are Creator of all things

You are the wind beneath my wings

You are the brilliance in my mind

You are the wisdom of my soul

You are my history

You are my destiny

You are the You that is in me

And I thank You for You, and who You are to me.

ABOUT THE AUTHOR

DR. DEE GREATHOUSE is a retired Army Warrant Officer and Veteran of the Gulf War, as well as an entrepreneur, teacher, author, radio host, and inspirational speaker. Among other responsibilities, she is the founder and President / CEO of What About Me Ministries, International Inc.; What About Me Music; The Sankofa Media Group; as well as Dr. Dee Greathouse Ministries based in Atlanta, Georgia.

Dr. Greathouse travels extensively teaching God's Word, utilizing her extensive background in the armed service, education, and more than 30 years of management and leadership skills, along with life experiences and personal encounters with the Holy Spirit. She teaches practical application from the Word of God in order to engage and empower God's people to transform their lives. Her primary goal is to affect people in such a positive way that it causes a renovation of thought and a compelling desire to change, to heal, and to walk in the fullness of life.

Dr. Greathouse is the mother of one brilliant daughter Teana, who is married to her talented son-in-law William Sr., and Nana to three wonderfully bright and anointed grandchildren, Jessica, William (TJ), and Miles.

Faith that is dormant has no rewards attached to it, but Faith that is alive—the benefits are innumerable... *That's my kind of Faith.*

—DR. DEE

CONTACT THE AUTHOR

Please contact the author at

Web:
deegreathouseministries.com

Email:
info@deegreathouseministries.com

Phone:
855-334-7316

Address:
207 Banks Station PMB #667
Fayetteville, GA 30214

Facebook:
https://www.facebook.com/deegreathouseministries

Twitter:
https://twitter.com/DeeGreathouse

Linkedin:
Dr. Delphine (Dee) Greathouse

Blogtalk Radio:
http://hosts.blogtalkradio.com/deegreat

REFLECTIONS

REFLECTIONS ARE LIKE the air that we breathe. With every breath we inhale our minds become more alert and engaged, and with every breath we exhale we have more strength to produce. When we reflect, we learn, examine, analyze, engage and once again we produce. From this book what has God revealed to you about Himself?

_____

_____

_____

_____

_____

_____

_____

_____

_____

_____

_____

_____

REFLECTIONS

REFLECTIONS

REFLECTIONS

REFLECTIONS

_____

_____

_____

_____

_____

_____

_____

_____

_____

_____

_____

_____

_____

_____

_____

_____

_____